ITALIAN PASTA

LONG

SHORT

FRESH AND FILLED

93 BEAUTIFULLY ILLUSTRATED, TESTED, STEP-BY-STEP RECIPES

THE MOST COMPLEX PROCEDURES EXPLAINED WITH
EASY-TO-FOLLOW PHOTOGRAPHS

EDITED BY ELISABETTA PIAZZESI

BONECHI

The photographs from the Bonechi Archives were taken by Andrea Fantauzzo.
The photograph from the Bonechi Archives on pages 104 was taken by Dario Grimoldi.

All the recipes in this book were tested by Elisabetta Piazzesi *and nutritionally analyzed by* Dr. John Luke Hili.

Project and editorial concept: Casa Editrice Bonechi
Editor: Paolo Piazzesi
Graphics and cover: Maria Rosanna Malagrinò
Video layout: Elena Nannucci
Editing: Federica Balloni
English translation: Julia Weiss

© Copyright by Casa Editrice Bonechi - Florence - Italy
E-mail: bonechi@bonechi.it

Printed in Italy by Centro Stampa Editoriale Bonechi, *Sesto Fiorentino.*

www.bonechi.com

INTRODUCTION

*P*asta, made by mixing flour and water and kneading until a compact dough is formed and then dried without fermenting is universally acknowledged as one of the tastiest and typical components of Mediterranean cuisine in general, and Italian cooking in particular. It is part of centuries of the peninsula's culinary traditions if it is true that it was already being handmade in many regions of Italy as early as the XIV century, and that by the nineteenth century the first artisan-type pasta factories opened their doors in Naples. Later, with the advent of mixing and kneading machines they were transformed into true industrial enterprises. In any event, the word "pasta" from the Greek "pàste" meaning "flour mixed with sauces" runs the risk of being too generic. It is used for a vast and complex range of products.

First of all, we must make a distinction between fresh, homemade egg pasta that is rolled out and set aside to dry, and plain, dry pasta in different shapes and sizes. The former is more typical of Northern Italian cuisine that leans towards meat, ricotta cheese, potato and vegetable fillings, creating agnolotti, tortellini *and* ravioli *to* flank the simplicity of tagliolini, tagliatelle *and* lasagna. *Using durum wheat alone to make the dough is typical of Southern Italian gastronomic traditions that favor dry pasta in its two main variations: short and long.*

Different names are used according to shape and size: spaghetti *and* rigatoni, tortiglioni *and* penne, mezzani *and* sedani, *while the famous word* macaroni *is used for both long and short varieties. Even the ways of cooking the two main types of pasta differ: dry pasta requires a large pot of water that you must salt when it reaches the boil, add the pasta and drain it when it is firm, but not crunchy, that is al dente. The cooking time is usually shown on the package (ranging from about 8 to 15 minutes). Fresh pasta also needs lots of water, but the cooking time varies significantly according to the complementary ingredients and whether or not there is any filling.*

*F*rom the nutritional stand-point fresh pasta, especially when filled, is a high-energy food containing all the nutrients of a full meal. For this reason, it can be considered a meal in itself, especially if it is enriched with an olive oil based condiment and a filling that provides fats, proteins, minerals and vitamins.

Dry pasta, on the other hand, the basis of the Mediterranean diet, like bread, rice and baked goods is a prime source of complex carbohydrates. It is a valid alternative to other starchy foods (100 g/4 oz of pasta is equivalent to the same quantity of rice, 120g/5 oz of bread and about 360g/13 oz of potatoes). At least one serving of pasta is recommended each day, even in reducing diets because of its low calorie content (360Kcal for every 100 g/4 oz).

Finally, whole wheat pasta deserves a little note. Since, like rice, it has a relatively low fiber content, it should not be considered compulsory, not even for treating constipation. If anything, it should be used as a tasty vehicle for vegetables according to the most classic form of the Mediterranean diet.

INFORMATION AND HELPFUL HINTS

*T*he completely original recipes in this book were selected and tested by a specially created team of professional chefs as you can see in the splendid color photographs. In parallel, they were analyzed for nutritional content by Dr. John Luke Hili. We carefully verified not only the final results, but also the various steps in preparation, cooking times and methods, the calories, proteins and nutritional content of each dish. In order not to waste such a valuable experience we decided to condense the information into a little table for each recipe. These flash cards list the ingredients, amounts and, at a glance, show how complicated each recipe is, along with calorie, protein and fat content. All the information for a tasty, nutritional diet is at your fingertips, to make meal planning easier and more fun. Cooking and preparation times are shown in minutes (e. g. 30'= thirty minutes).

Next to the title of each recipe you will see the appropriate cooking vessel:

 SAUCEPAN – *round, with a lid, for medium-long stove-top cooking; the diameter of 25-30 cm (9-11 inches) is greater than the depth.*

SKILLET – *round with low, (maximum 10 cm/3 inches) curved sides with a long handle for frying, sautéing or preparing bases and sauces.*

 POT – *round, with a lid, for boiling water or other liquids, cooking pasta, soups, meats and vegetables; pots are deeper than they are wide.*

 PAN – *round, with low sides (max. 6 cm/2 1/2 inches high) for slowly cooking sauces.*

 OVEN PANS AND DISHES – *size and shape vary, they are made of metal (usually coated aluminum), porcelain or glass, with lids and are used for oven-baking.*

How to read the *FLASH* cards

PREPARATION TIME
COOKING TIME
DIFFICULTY
SERVINGS
FLAVOR

- EASY
- MEDIUM
- DIFFICULT

🕐 20' ❀ 15' 4

DELICATE ★
PRONOUNCED ★★
HEARTY ★★★

350g/13 oz Bavettine
120g/5 oz
Mascarpone
1 Lemon
Basil
Marjoram

KILOCALORIES (per serving)

NUTRITIONAL VALUE

Kcal 483 P 10 F 25

LOW
MEDIUM
HIGH

PROTEINS (per serving)
FATS (per serving)

TABLE OF CONTENTS

Introduction 3
Information
    and Helpful Hints 5

Long Pasta 9
Short Pasta 43
Fresh and Filled Pasta 83

LONG PASTA

Bavettine with cheese
    and mushrooms 10
Bavettine with lemon and cheese 10
Linguine in pink sauce 17
Linguine with four cheeses 17
Linguine with frankfurters 15
Linguine with scallops 12
Linguine with zucchini blossoms 15

Perciatelli with tuna fish
    and tomato sauce 18
Smoked spaghettini 28
Spaghetti all'amatriciana 24
Spaghetti baked in foil 22
Spaghetti Maratea 20
Spaghetti Miseno 26
Spaghetti with black olives 25
Spaghetti with shrimp 21
Spaghettini Teulada 28
Spaghettini with spicy vegetables 30
Spaghettini with white clam sauce 31
Tagliolini with caviar 32
Trenette di Ponente 37
Trenette with pesto 34
Trenette with tuna in white sauce 36
Trinette generose 39
Trinette with spinach 38
Vermicelli Bella Napoli 40
Vermicelli with asparagus 40

SHORT PASTA

Chiocciole Campidano 44
Chiocciole Santarosa 45
Conchiglie with tomato sauce 46
Conchigliette Brabante 49
Conchigliette with eggplant 48
Farfalle Cézanne 52
Farfalle with asparagus and béchamel 50
Farfalle with smoked salmon 51
Fusilli Smoking 54
Fusilli Velouté 56
Fusilli with tomatoes and bacon 55
Maccheroncetti with smoked bacon 59
Maccheroni alla Norma 59

Sedani with beans 74
Sedani with fennel and tomatoes 70
Sedani with shrimp and mushrooms 77
Sweet sedani 76
Tortiglioni Piedigrotta 78
Tortiglioni with clams 80
Tortiglioni with zucchini 79

Mezzani alla Luciana 62
Mezzani au gratin 62
Mezzani Capodimonte 61
Mezzani fricassee 60
Orecchiette with broccoli 64
Pasta with sardines 65
Penne Barcarola 66
Penne with baby octopus 66
Pennette with rabbit 68
Poor man's pennette 69
Rigatoni al fresco 73
Rigatoni Marinella 72
Sedani di Vinicio 75

FRESH AND FILLED PASTA

Agnolini in broth 84
Agnolotti in meat sauce 86
Bavette timbale 88
Bread gnocchi 99
Cannelloni with mushrooms 90
Classic tortellini 126
Gnocchetti with codfish 97
Gnocchi with nettles 99
Gourmet's timbale 120
Green and white lasagne 100
Green lasagne 102
Green ravioli 110
Making egg pasta 85
Nastrini alla pizzaiola 96
Pansotti with walnuts 104
Pappardelle with duck 106
Pappardelle with hare sauce 107
Pappardelle with mutton 105
Ravioli in ginger sauce 110
Ravioli Southern Style 113
Ravioli with green beans 108
Rich tortellini 125
Sicilian cannelloni 92
Springtime noodle loaf 114
Strascinati with lamb sauce 117
Striscioni with thyme 113
Super cannelloni 95
Tagliatelle, taglierini & c. 89

Tagliatelle with ham 117
Tagliolini timbale 118
Tortelli in broth 124
Tortelli with potato filling 122
Tortelli with squash filling 121
Two-Flavor Ravioli 108
Vincisgrassi 119

LONG PASTA

Bavette with lemon and cheese ►

Finely chop the herbs. Wash the lemon and grate the zest – be careful not to grate the white cellulose part. Put the mascarpone cheese into the serving bowl, add 2 tablespoons olive oil, the chopped herbs and the grated lemon zest. Blend the ingredients well to obtain a smooth mixture, add salt and pepper to taste and set the bowl aside in a warm place.

Cook the bavettini *al dente*, drain and put them into the bowl with the cheese mixture, add one tablespoon of the cooking water. Stir gently, garnish with a few whole thyme and marjoram leaves. Serve hot.

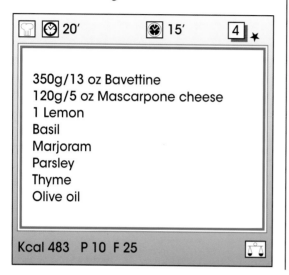

🍳 ⏰ 20'   ❀ 15'   4 ★

350g/13 oz Bavettine
120g/5 oz Mascarpone cheese
1 Lemon
Basil
Marjoram
Parsley
Thyme
Olive oil

Kcal 483   P 10   F 25

A sprinkling of parmesan cheese is option (but in our prejudiced opinion, the delicate combination of herbs and the mascarpone makes any more cheese superfluous if not undesirable).

Bavettine with cheese and mushrooms

To start, put the dried mushrooms in a small bowl, cover with lukewarm water and let them soak for about 30 minutes. Drain and squeeze out the excess water. Put the water through a fine sieve and set aside.

Crush the garlic and sauté it in a skillet with 2-3 tablespoons olive oil. As soon as the garlic starts to brown remove it and add the mushrooms. Add salt and pepper to taste. Cook for 10 minutes over a medium flame (if it gets dry, add a little of the mushroom water, or a drop of white wine if you prefer), add the parsley. In the meantime, cook the pasta. Crumble the ricotta cheese into the serving bowl, add the mushroom sauce and mix thoroughly with a wooden spoon.

Drain the pasta when it is *al dente* and put it in the bowl; mix quickly and serve immediately. There is no need to add parmesan cheese, see the comments for the preceding recipe.

Bavette *or* bavettine *are very similar to* linguine, *about 25 cm (9 inches) long, not more than 3 mm (1/4 inch) wide and 1 mm (1/16 inch) thick.*

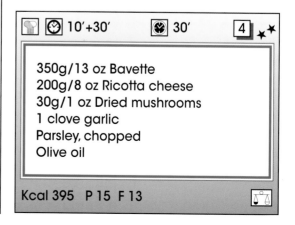

🍳 ⏰ 10'+30'   ❀ 30'   4 ★★

350g/13 oz Bavette
200g/8 oz Ricotta cheese
30g/1 oz Dried mushrooms
1 clove garlic
Parsley, chopped
Olive oil

Kcal 395   P 15   F 13

Linguine with scallops

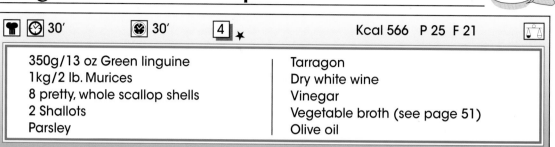

| 🍴 🕐 30′ | ⚙ 30′ | 4 ★ | Kcal 566 P 25 F 21 | ⚖ |

350g/13 oz Green linguine	Tarragon
1kg/2 lb. Murices	Dry white wine
8 pretty, whole scallop shells	Vinegar
2 Shallots	Vegetable broth (see page 51)
Parsley	Olive oil

1 Scald the murices in water with a small glass of vinegar. Use a toothpick to remove them from the shells. Set aside a few of the shells for garnish.

3 Chop the shallots, sauté gently in 2-3 tablespoons olive oil, add the murices and stir. Add one glass of dry white wine, when the wine has evaporated cook for 10 minutes adding broth.

2 Brush the scallop shells clean and open them, making sure to remove all the sand.
Put the white and orange parts of the flesh into a bowl and rinse, change the water and rinse several times.
Put the concave part of the shells aside for serving.

4 Add the orange and white flesh, salt and pepper to taste and cook for about 2 minutes.
In the meantime, cook the linguine *al dente*. Drain and dress with the sauce, sprinkle with chopped parsley and tarragon. Put helpings of pasta onto the shells and garnish as you like.

Linguine with zucchini blossoms ◀

Wash the zucchini blossoms and pat dry with paper towels.

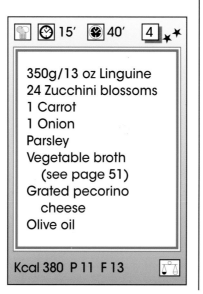

🍳 🕐 15′ 🕐 40′ 4 ★★

350g/13 oz Linguine
24 Zucchini blossoms
1 Carrot
1 Onion
Parsley
Vegetable broth
   (see page 51)
Grated pecorino
   cheese
Olive oil

Kcal 380 P 11 F 13 ⚖

Set aside four blossoms to garnish the plates, and cut the others into strips.
Clean the onion and carrot, chop finely and sauté in a skillet with 4-5 tablespoons olive oil.
Add salt and pepper and a ladle of broth.
Cook over a low flame for about 15 min, then add the zucchini blossoms, stir and cook for 6-7 minutes.
In the meantime, cook the pasta *al dente*, drain and dress with the sauce. Sprinkle with chopped parsley and grated pecorino cheese.

Linguine with frankfurters

Put the pasta on to cook. Wash and chop the parsley, remove the skin from the frankfurters and cut them into little disks.
In a skillet, melt the butter and brown the frankfurter slices over a low flame with a pinch of salt and tarragon.
Put the cream cheese in your serving bowl, mix in the frankfurter slices, add a dash of pepper (or a tablespoon of sweet paprika).
Drain the pasta when it is *al dente* and add it to the serving bowl, sprinkle with parsley.

Mix and serve with lots of grated parmesan cheese.

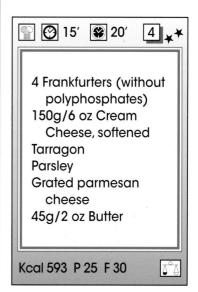

🍳 🕐 15′ 🕐 20′ 4 ★★

4 Frankfurters (without
   polyphosphates)
150g/6 oz Cream
   Cheese, softened
Tarragon
Parsley
Grated parmesan
   cheese
45g/2 oz Butter

Kcal 593 P 25 F 30 ⚖

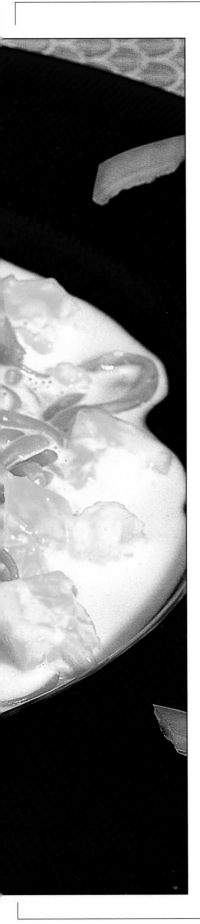

Linguine with four cheeses ◄

Heat a ladle of cream in a double boiler, add the butter along with a pinch of salt and a dash of pepper.

Keep this mixture warm. Put the pasta on to cook.

In the meantime, cut the hard cheeses into little cubes and put them in your serving bowl.

Drain the linguine *al dente* and immediately place in the bowl with the cheese cubes; dress with half the cream-and-butter mixture and grated parmesan cheese. Toss to mix well, before serving add the rest of the cream-and-butter and more grated parmesan.

🍳 ⏱ 10′ ❄ 20′ 4 ★★

350g/13 oz Green linguine
80g/3 oz Mozzarella cheese
80g/3 oz Emmenthal cheese
80g/3 oz Edam cheese
Grated parmesan cheese
Heavy cream
50g/2 oz Butter

Kcal 675 P 27 F 37

Linguine in pink sauce

🍳 ⏱ 10′ ❄ 30′ 4 ★★

350g/13 oz Linguine
1 Shallot
Tomato purée
Heavy cream
Grated parmesan cheese
40g/1.5 oz Butter

Kcal 515 P 13 F 25

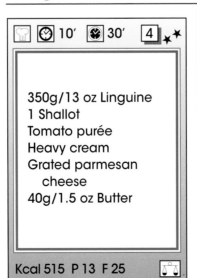

Clean the shallot and chop it finely.

Gently sauté it in melted butter. Add about one ladle of tomato purée, salt and stir.

After about 6-8 minutes turn off the flame and add 2-3 tablespoons cream, stir gently to blend thoroughly.

Cook the linguine and drain when they are still very *al dente*. Put the pasta into the skillet, and cook over a low flame for a few minutes. Serve with grated parmesan cheese.

Perciatelli with tuna fish and tomato sauce

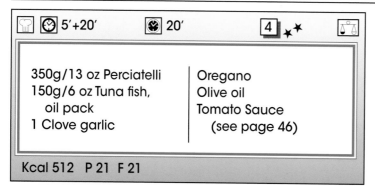

350g/13 oz Perciatelli	Oregano
150g/6 oz Tuna fish, oil pack	Olive oil
1 Clove garlic	Tomato Sauce (see page 46)

Kcal 512 P 21 F 21

Sauté the garlic in a skillet with 2-3 tablespoons olive oil. Remove the garlic, add the tuna fish, crumbled. After 2-3 minutes add 2 ladles of tomato sauce (see instructions on page 46), salt and pepper. Stir and cook for a couple of minutes. Cook the pasta *al dente*, drain dress with the sauce and sprinkle with oregano. Grated parmesan cheese is definitely not recommended!

Spaghetti Maratea

S cald the calamary and shrimp in separate pans; in the meantime, put the clams and fasolari in a skillet with a squiggle of olive oil and a splash of white wine, cook over a high flame until the shells open. When they are ready – it will take a few minutes – remove the shells and strain the liquid. Make sure that you eliminate all the sand. Cut the peppers into strips.

Sauté the garlic in 4-5 tablespoons olive oil, remove it from the skillet when it starts to brown, add the clams, fasolari, calamary and shrimp cut into pieces, the peppers, salt and pepper.

Cook over a medium flame for 10 minutes and moisten with the liquid from the clams.

In the meantime cook the spaghetti and drain just before they are *al dente*. Slide the spaghetti into the skillet and cook over a moderate flame for a few minutes. Sprinkle with chopped parsley and remember – no cheese!

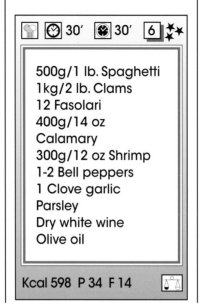

🍳 ⏱ 30′ ⏰ 30′ 6 ✦✦

500g/1 lb. Spaghetti
1kg/2 lb. Clams
12 Fasolari
400g/14 oz Calamary
300g/12 oz Shrimp
1-2 Bell peppers
1 Clove garlic
Parsley
Dry white wine
Olive oil

Kcal 598 P 34 F 14

Spaghetti with shrimp

Scald the shrimp in slightly salted boiling water for 5-6 minutes. Drain, shell and remove the black vein. Sauté the garlic in 5-6 tablespoons olive oil and remove it from the skillet when it starts to brown.

Add the shrimp, pour in a glass of white wine and let it evaporate over a high flame. Add salt, pepper and half a ladle of vegetable broth; simmer over a moderate flame for 10 minutes.

Cook the pasta *al dente* drain, and turn it into the skillet. Toss gently, without crushing the shrimp, so that it absorbs all the flavor.

Garnish with chopped parsley and serve.

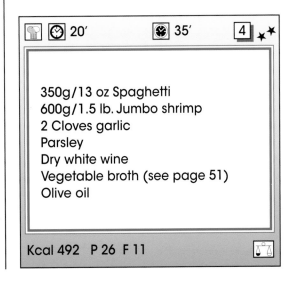

🕛 20'   ✹ 35'   4 ★★

350g/13 oz Spaghetti
600g/1.5 lb. Jumbo shrimp
2 Cloves garlic
Parsley
Dry white wine
Vegetable broth (see page 51)
Olive oil

Kcal 492   P 26   F 11

Spaghetti baked in foil

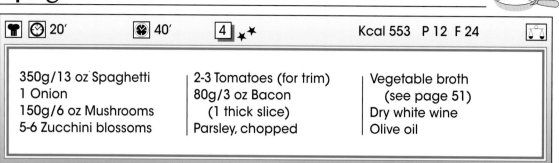

🍴 ⏱ 20′	❋ 40′	4 ✦★	Kcal 553 P 12 F 24	⚖

350g/13 oz Spaghetti	2-3 Tomatoes (for trim)	Vegetable broth
1 Onion	80g/3 oz Bacon	(see page 51)
150g/6 oz Mushrooms	(1 thick slice)	Dry white wine
5-6 Zucchini blossoms	Parsley, chopped	Olive oil

1 Clean the zucchini blossoms and set aside. Wash the mushrooms under running water, dry and slice thinly. Cut the onion into thin rings and sauté in 4-5 tablespoons olive oil. Add 1/2 glass white wine and let the wine evaporate.

3 Cook the spaghetti and drain when about 4/5 cooked – that is about 6-7 minutes of cooking time. Put the spaghetti in a bowl and dress with the mushroom sauce; mix well.

2 Add the bacon, cut into bits; when it is browned, add the mushrooms and the parsley. Add salt, pepper and a little broth; cook slowly for 20 minutes.

4 Place the pasta on a sheet of heavy duty aluminum foil, add the zucchini blossoms. Close the foil and bake in a hot oven (200-220°C/400-430°F) for about 5 minutes. Remove from the oven, open the foil to let the steam escape and garnish with two tomatoes. Serve immediately.

Spaghetti all'amatriciana

Wash the tomatoes, cut them in half, remove the seeds, and cut into chunks. Clean the onion and slice it thinly. Sauté the onion in 4 tablespoons olive oil, and add the bacon cut into bits.

Then add the tomatoes and cook over a low flame for just 15 minutes.

Add salt and pepper to taste. In the meantime, cook the pasta *al dente*, drain and put into a serving bowl. Top with the sauce and toss.

Serve with a generous sprinkling of pecorino. This tasty condiment can also be made with smoked bacon.

🍳 ⏱ 15' ❄ 30' 4 ★★

350g/13 oz Spaghetti or bucatini
1 Onion
80g/3 oz Fatback or streaky bacon (one thick slice)
4-5 Ripe tomatoes
Aged pecorino cheese
Olive oil

Kcal 527 P 13 F 27

Spaghetti with black olives

Pit the olives and cut them in half. Sauté one clove of crushed garlic along with the chili pepper in 5-6 tablespoons olive oil.

When the garlic starts to brown, remove it along with the chili pepper and add the olives, drained capers and the other, whole clove of garlic and cook over a lively flame for 3-4 minutes. At this point, you can add the anchovy (washed, filleted and cut into pieces) if you like.

Cook the spaghetti and drain it while it is very much *al dente*, turn it into the skillet, stir and sprinkle with chopped parsley. Cheese is not a must on this dish.

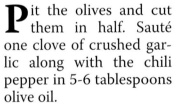

| 🍳 | ⏱ 15′ | ✺ 20′ | 4 ✷✷ | Kcal 389   P 8   F 15 | ⚖ |

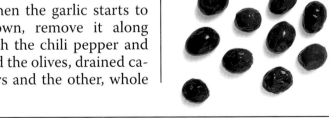

350g/13 oz Spaghetti	Capers in vinegar	1 Anchovy (optional)
2 Cloves garlic	Chili pepper	Olive oil
Black olives	Parsley	

Spaghetti Miseno

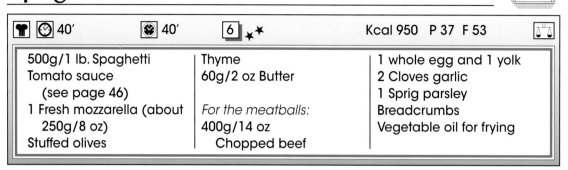

🍽 ⏰ 40′	❁ 40′	6 ✦★	Kcal 950 P 37 F 53	⚖

500g/1 lb. Spaghetti
Tomato sauce
   (see page 46)
1 Fresh mozzarella (about
   250g/8 oz)
Stuffed olives
	Thyme
	60g/2 oz Butter
	
	For the meatballs:
	400g/14 oz
	   Chopped beef
		1 whole egg and 1 yolk
		2 Cloves garlic
		1 Sprig parsley
		Breadcrumbs
		Vegetable oil for frying

1 In a mixing bowl, combine the meat, whole egg and yolk, chopped garlic and parsley. Blend well; shape little meatballs and coat with breadcrumbs.

3 Cook the spaghetti for 6-7 minutes and drain. Dress with the tomato sauce, add the meatballs, the olives – cut in half – and the mozzarella cut into strips. Garnish with thyme leaves.

2 Fry the meatballs in hot oil over a moderate flame. Remove them as they are done using a slotted spoon and drain them on paper towels.

4 Put the dressed spaghetti into a baking dish and top with melted butter. Bake at 200°C/400°F for 8-10 minutes, until the mozzarella starts to melt.

Smoked spaghettini

🍽 ⏰ 15′   ❂ 30′   4 ✦✦

350g/13 oz Spaghetti
100 g/4 oz Smoked bacon
   (1 slice)
3-4 Ripe tomatoes
1 Clove garlic
1 Chili pepper
Olive oil

Kcal 489 P 10 F 24

Wash the tomatoes, cut them in half, remove the seeds and cut them into cubes. Crush the garlic and sauté it in 4-5 tablespoons olive oil. Remove it when it starts to brown, add the tomatoes and the whole chili pepper. Cook for a few minutes and then add the bacon, cut into little bits.

Salt to taste and cook over a low flame for 15 minutes. If it tends to dry, add half a ladle of warm water. Cook the spaghettini for 5-6 minutes and drain; turn into the skillet – make sure to remove the chili pepper – and cook over a low flame until they are *al dente*. Cheese is optional.

Spaghettini Teulada

While the spaghettini is cooking, crush the garlic and sauté it, together with the whole chili pepper in a skillet with 5-6 tablespoons olive oil.
Remove the garlic as soon as it starts to brown, add the finely crumbled roe and a sprig of chopped parsley and cook for a couple of minutes. Drain the pasta while it is still very much *al dente*, transfer it to the skillet and sauté it quickly in the sauce over a high flame; remove the skillet as soon as it starts to sizzle. Cheese is just not the right thing on this dish!.

Here is another pasta dressing that is fast and very tasty. If you have a few extra minutes, clean a carrot and a stalk of celery. Slice the celery into strips and julienne the carrot. Add it to the condiment together with the pasta –and buon appetito.

🍽 ⏰ 5′   ❂ 15′   4 ✦✦

350g/13 oz Spaghettini
150 Mullet roe
1 Clove garlic
Parsley
Chili pepper
Olive oil

Kcal 391 P 14 F 13

Real "bottarga", a delicacy, consists of mullet roe that has been salted, pressed and aged for about 4 months.
It is also made with bass roe; the version made of tuna or codfish roe is less delicately flavored.

Spaghettini with spicy vegetables

🍳 ⏱ 20'   ✹ 40'   4 ✦✦

350g/13 oz Spaghettini
1 Carrot
1 Onion
2-3 Zucchini
2-3 Ripe tomatoes
2 Chili peppers
Vegetable broth (see page 51)
Parsley
Olive oil

Kcal 366   P 9 F 11

finely; sauté them in a skillet in 4-5 tablespoons olive oil along with the whole chili peppers.

Add the zucchini, salt and pepper to taste; add a ladle of broth and cook for 10 minutes. Add the tomatoes, cut into chunks and simmer for 10 minutes more.

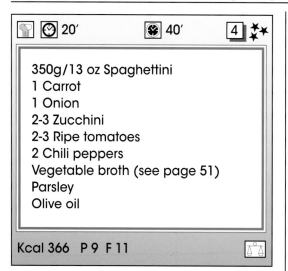

Wash the tomatoes, cut them open and remove the seeds. Wash the zucchini and slice them into disks. Wash the carrot and onion and chop them

Cook the spaghettini for 5-6 minutes, drain; add to the skillet (remember to remove the chili peppers) and cook over a low flame, stirring gently, until they are *al dente*. Serve with a sprinkling of chopped parsley. You do not need cheese on this at all.

Spaghettini with white clam sauce

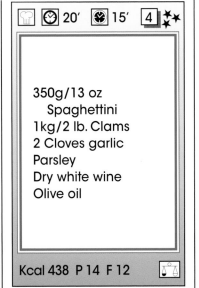

Place the clams in a skillet along with one clove of garlic, crushed, a sprig of parsley, a little olive oil and half a glass of white wine.

Cover the skillet and cook over a high flame until the clams open; remove from the stove and strain the liquid, eliminating any solid residue.

Put the clams back in the skillet with the strained liquid, one clove garlic and a sprig of parsley, finely chopped, add a pinch of salt and pepper: keep warm.

Cook the pasta for 5-6

⬛ 🕐 20′ 🕐 15′ 4 ✦✦

350g/13 oz
  Spaghettini
1kg/2 lb. Clams
2 Cloves garlic
Parsley
Dry white wine
Olive oil

Kcal 438 P 14 F 12

minutes; place it in the skillet and let it absorb the flavors by stirring gently;

remove when it is *al dente*. Remove the garlic and serve with a sprinkling of chopped parsley.

Cheese? Don't even think about it!

If you want to make this fantastic dish even better, use 500g/1 lb. clams, and 500g/1 lb. mussels; then when you are about to put the pasta into the skillet, add one ripe tomato, cut into little cubes.

Tagliolini with caviar

Wash the salmon, remove the skin and chop it. Wash the shallots, chop them finely. Melt the butter in a skillet, over a low flame and slowly sauté the chopped shallots. Add the salmon, salt and pepper to taste and moisten with half a glass of spumante.

After 5-6 minutes remove the skillet from the stove, put the salmon into the blender. Put the mixture back into the skillet, set aside and keep warm.
Cook the tagliolini and drain well before they are *al dente*, and turn them into the skillet, sprinkle with the caviar and serve immediately. Garnish the plates with parsley leaves and lemon slices. Absolutely no cheese allowed!

🕒 15'   ✺ 20'   4 ★★

350g/13 oz Tagliolini
200g/8 oz Fresh salmon (1 slice)
50g/2 oz Caviar
2-3 Shallots
Dry spumante
Parsley (for garnish)
1 Lemon (for garnish)
60g/2 oz Butter

Kcal 466   P 19   F 13

Trenette with pesto

| 🍴 ⏱ 15′ | ⏰ 12′ | 4 ★✦ | Kcal 770 P 24 F 48 | ⚖ |

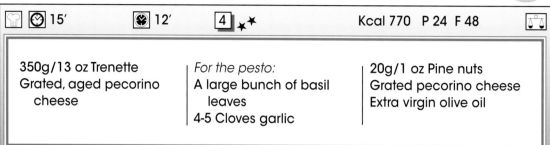

350g/13 oz Trenette
Grated, aged pecorino
cheese

For the pesto:
A large bunch of basil
leaves
4-5 Cloves garlic

20g/1 oz Pine nuts
Grated pecorino cheese
Extra virgin olive oil

Cook the trenette *al dente*, and drain; put two ladles of pesto (see instructions below) into a bowl add the trenette and cover with another two ladles of pesto, and mix. Serve with a dish of grated pecorino on the side.

1 Rinse the basil under cold running water, dry well between two clean dishcloths.

2 Put the basil, the peeled garlic and the pine nuts into the blender bowl; process at low speed until it becomes a thick paste.

3 Add the grated pecorino – the cheese should not be too aged nor too salty – and process for a few seconds at medium speed.

4 Put the pesto into a bowl and gradually add olive oil, mixing constantly with a wooden spoon until it becomes fluid. Let it stand a bit before using.

You can store pesto for 2-3 weeks in hermetically sealed glass jars by topping it with olive oil. Keep the jars in a dark place.

Trenette with tuna in white sauce

Wash the anchovies under cold, running water, filet, bone and break into little bits. Drain the tuna fish and crumble it. Sauté the garlic in a skillet with 3-4 tablespoons olive oil; remove the garlic and add the tuna and anchovies. Moisten with half a glass of white wine, cook slowly then salt and pepper to taste. Let the mixture simmer for 10 minutes, stirring gently from time to time.

In the meantime, cook the trenette, *al dente*, drain and dress with the sauce and garnish with parsley before serving.

Trenette *are shaped more or less like* bavette, *are lightly wider and thicker.* Trenette *are a specialty of the Liguria region of Italy.*

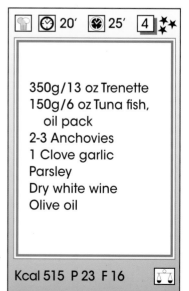

🍲 ⏱ 20′ ❀ 25′ 4 ✹✹

350g/13 oz Trenette
150g/6 oz Tuna fish, oil pack
2-3 Anchovies
1 Clove garlic
Parsley
Dry white wine
Olive oil

Kcal 515 P 23 F 16

Trenette di Ponente

🍳 ⏲ 20′ ⏰ 30′ [4] ★★

350g/13 oz Trenette
300g/12 oz Shrimp
1 Green onion
   (or 1 shallot)
Cream
Marjoram, parsley
   and thyme
60g/2 oz Butter

Kcal 465 P 17 F 20

Scald the shrimp for 2-3 minutes, drain and shell; be sure to remove the black vein.

Set a few shrimp aside for trim.

Clean and chop the onion and sauté it in melted butter. Add the shrimp, half a ladle of cream and a few springs of thyme and marjoram.

Salt and pepper to taste, cook for about 10 minutes until the sauce thickens while stirring continuously.

Cook the trenette *al dente*, drain, turn them into the skillet, stir and cook briefly over a medium flame so they absorb the flavors.

Serve the pasta garnished with parsley leaves and the whole shrimp. Do not add cheese.

Trinette with spinach

Scald the spinach in boiling water, drain, squeeze out excess water and chop.

Cut the speck into cubes. Sauté the crushed garlic and the chili pepper in 5-6 tablespoons olive oil. Remove the garlic as soon as it starts to brown, remove the chili pepper too.

Add the spinach, speck and half a ladle of cream.

In the meantime cook the trinette.

Drain when they are four fifths cooked and turn them into the skillet, and sprinkle with flaked provolone, continue cooking slowly until the pasta is *al dente*.

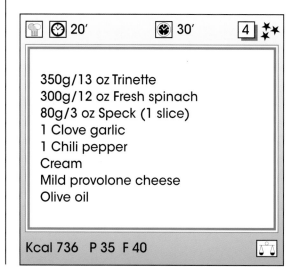

20′   30′   4 ✹✹

350g/13 oz Trinette
300g/12 oz Fresh spinach
80g/3 oz Speck (1 slice)
1 Clove garlic
1 Chili pepper
Cream
Mild provolone cheese
Olive oil

Kcal 736   P 35   F 40

Trinette generose

Rinse the anchovies under cold, running water, filet and break them up into little pieces. Cut the mozzarella into small cubes.

In your serving bowl, beat the egg yolks, add the anchovies and mozzarella, salt and pepper to taste. In the meantime, put the trinette on to cook, drain when they are *al dente*. Pour the melted butter into the serving bowl and then add the trinette. Stir briskly so that the mozzarella melts and the egg coats the pasta. Serve immediately without any other cheese.

Trinette *(which are also called* reginette*) are about 1 to 3 mm (1/4 inch) wide with curly edges. They are also available made with eggs.*

🍳 ⏲ 15′ ❀ 20′ 4 ★★

350g/13 oz Trinette
1 Fresh, water-pack
    mozzarella cheese
4 Anchovies
3 Egg yolks
Bay leaves (for trim)
50g/2 oz Butter

Kcal 582 P 28 F 27

Vermicelli Bella Napoli

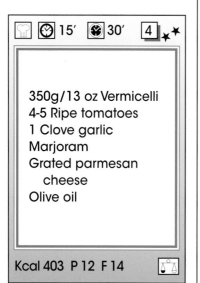

🍴 ⏲ 15' ✺ 30' 4 ★ ★

350g/13 oz Vermicelli
4-5 Ripe tomatoes
1 Clove garlic
Marjoram
Grated parmesan
  cheese
Olive oil

Kcal 403 P 12 F 14

Sauté the crushed garlic in a skillet with 5-6 tablespoons olive oil. Remove the garlic as soon as it starts to brown, and add the tomatoes, cut into chunks. Salt and pepper to taste and let the tomatoes simmer for about 20 minutes.

Cook the pasta *al dente*, drain, put into a serving bowl and dress with the tomato sauce.

Add a generous sprinkling of grated parmesan cheese and garnish the plates with fresh marjoram leaves.

Vermicelli with asparagus

Tie the asparagus into a bunch and cook covered for 15 minutes. Drain and cut off the tough part of the stems; cut the rest into bits. Slice the artichokes thinly. Slice the onion and sauté it in a skillet with 4-5 tablespoons olive oil, add the artichokes, salt and pepper to taste.

Add a ladle of vegetable broth and cook over a lively flame until the liquid is absorbed. Cook the vermicelli and drain before they are *al dente*. Turn them into the skillet along with the asparagus, add a sprig of chopped parsley. Cook over a low flame for a few minutes and serve with lots of grated parmesan cheese.

🍴 ⏲ 25' ✺ 30'+15' 4 ★ ★

350g/13 oz Vermicelli
12 Asparagus
4 Artichokes
1 Green onion
  (or 1 shallot)
1 Lemon
Parsley
Vegetable broth
  (see page 51)
Grated parmesan
  cheese
Olive oil

Kcal 435 P 15 F 14

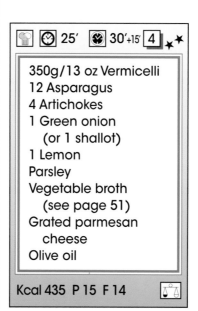

SHORT PASTA

Chiocciole Campidano

Rinse the anchovies under cold running water, remove the heads, bone and filet.

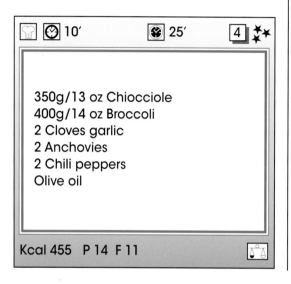

🍳 ⏱ 10'   ✿ 25'   4 ✨✨

350g/13 oz Chiocciole
400g/14 oz Broccoli
2 Cloves garlic
2 Anchovies
2 Chili peppers
Olive oil

Kcal 455 P 14 F 11

Clean the broccoli and scald *al dente* in lots of slightly salted boiling water (test for doneness with a fork). Drain and set the water aside. Cut the broccoli flowers into little pieces.

Sauté the garlic in a skillet with 3-4 tablespoons olive oil, then remove it.

Turn the broccoli and the chopped chili peppers into the skillet and cook slowly for 5-6 minutes. In the meantime, put the pasta on to cook in the broccoli water. Drain the pasta just before it reaches the *al dente* point, turn into the skillet along with the anchovies, cook over a high flame for one minute, stirring vigorously with a wooden spoon.

Cheese is not really compulsory here, but if you do want some, use pecorino.

Chiocciole Santarosa

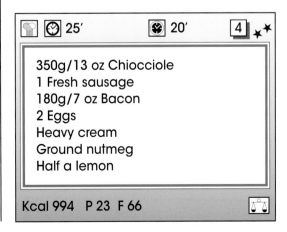

Remove the skin from the sausage and crumble it, sauté the meat and the bacon – cut into bits - in a skillet with a bit of water (water is often much better than oil when it comes to cooking pork). Beat the eggs in a large bowl, add a pinch of salt, pepper and nutmeg, as well as half a glass of heavy cream. Set aside.

Slice the lemon, then cut the slices into tiny little bits, set aside. Cook the pasta and drain before it is *al dente*, then turn it into the skillet. Cook for 2 minutes, stirring with a wooden spoon, then turn the contents of the skillet into the bowl. Add the lemon bits and toss gently.

Let the dressed pasta sit for 2-3 minutes, then serve. Since there is already cream, we do not recommend using cheese, but if you do, it should be pecorino.

🕑 25′	❈ 20′	4 ★✦

350g/13 oz Chiocciole
1 Fresh sausage
180g/7 oz Bacon
2 Eggs
Heavy cream
Ground nutmeg
Half a lemon

Kcal 994   P 23   F 66

Conchiglie with tomato sauce

🍳 ⏱ 15′	❄ 1h 40′	6 ★ ⭐	Kcal 539 P 15 F 19	⚖

500g/1 lb. Conchiglie
Butter and grated
   parmesan cheese
   (optional)
	For the tomato sauce:
	1kg/2 lb. Ripe tomatoes
	1 Carrot
	1 onion
	1 Stalk celery
		1 Clove garlic (optional)
		Chili pepper (optional)
		Parsley, basil
		Coarse salt, sugar
		Olive oil

This is probably one of the best and most reliable recipes for making exquisite tomato sauce.

1 Gather the ingredients. Clean and wash the vegetables and herbs. Chop up the tomatoes, and slice the carrot, onion and celery.

2 Put the vegetables into a saucepan along with the garlic and chili pepper (if you like); do not add water. Cook over a very low flame and gradually add a generous amount of coarse salt.

3 Cook over a moderate flame, covered if necessary, for about 45 minutes. Add a squiggle of olive oil, and cook for 30 minutes more.

4 Remove the sauce from the stove, put it through a food mill, and remove the tomato skins. Put it back on the stove and cook for 15 minutes. Turn off the flame, add sugar, chopped parsley and basil and let it sit; if you like, you can add another squiggle of olive oil.

Cook the conchiglie *al dente* and drain. Dress with the tomato sauce, add a pat of butter (if you like) and grated parmesan cheese. Remember: no butter, no cheese!

Conchigliette with eggplant

There are chefs who recommend that you slice and salt the eggplant, then put a weight (never wood or metal) over it to release the juices that may be bitter. This also prevents it from turning black. Then there are those, like us, who think all this is unnecessary and that eggplant is delicious just the way it is. But...we believe that you should be free to do as you like.

Scald and peel the tomatoes. Wash the eggplant and the chili peppers, and cut them into chunks.
Clean the onion and slice it thinly, then sauté it, with the garlic, in a skillet with 4-5 tablespoons olive oil.
Add the eggplant and chili peppers and cook for 5-6 minutes. Add the tomatoes and cook 10-12 minutes more over a medium flame.

Cook the conchigliette *al dente*, and drain. Turn them into the skillet, add 3-4 basil leaves and cook over a brisk flame, stirring with a wooden spoon.
Serve immediately.

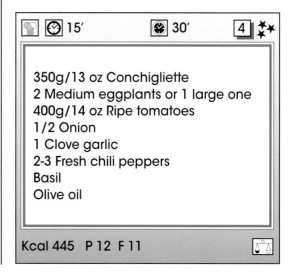

🕑 15'   ❀ 30'   4 ✵✶

350g/13 oz Conchigliette
2 Medium eggplants or 1 large one
400g/14 oz Ripe tomatoes
1/2 Onion
1 Clove garlic
2-3 Fresh chili peppers
Basil
Olive oil

Kcal 445   P 12   F 11

Conchigliette Brabante

W ash the Brussels sprouts, score the bottom of each with an "x", and cook for 10 minutes in lots of salted boiling water. Drain and set the water aside (you will use it to cook the pasta).

🍳	🕐 40'+30'	❀ 15'	4 ★

350g/13 oz Conchigliette
300g/12 oz Brussels sprouts
Ground Nutmeg
White wine vinegar (optional)
Grated parmesan cheese
60g/2 oz Butter

Kcal 494   P 16 F 16

Cut the sprouts into quarters and slowly cook them in a skillet with melted butter, a dash of ground white pepper and ground nutmeg, if you like the flavor, you can add a few drops of vinegar.
In the meantime, cook the conchigliette *al dente*, drain. Turn the pasta into the skillet and cook over a lively flame, stirring with a wooden spoon. Serve with a generous sprinkling of grated parmesan cheese.

Farfalle with asparagus and béchamel

Wash the asparagus thoroughly, make sure to remove all traces of soil. Tie them into a bunch and cook them, standing upright, in a pot. The water should only be slighted salted and should cover the white part of the stems. Cook them *al dente*, test with a fork, then drain. Strain the water and set it aside – you will add it to the water for cooking the pasta. Cut off the tough part of the stems, and chop up the rest. Leave a few tips whole, for garnish. Prepare the béchamel. In a saucepan, melt 40g/1,5 oz butter over a low flame, add the flour a little at a time, stirring constantly in the same direction. When the flour is golden, add a glass of milk, a little at a time – stirring all the while – a pinch of salt, pepper and ground nutmeg. When the sauce thickens remove it from the stove and mix in the egg yolk. Put the pasta on to cook. In the meantime, heat the asparagus in the rest of the melted butter in a skillet; add a dash of ground white pepper. Drain the pasta before it is *al dente* and turn it into the skillet, cook over a medium flame. Turn off the stove, add the béchamel sauce and toss gently.

Serve the pasta lukewarm, garnished with the whole asparagus tips. Grated parmesan cheese is not compulsory, but it is acceptable.

🍽 🕐 10′ ❋ 40′ 4 ★

350g/13 oz Farfalle
600g/1.5 lb. Asparagus
1 Egg yolk
80g/3 oz Butter

For the Béchamel Sauce:
Milk
50g/2 oz Flour
Ground Nutmeg
40g/1,5 oz Butter

Kcal 638 P 23 F 20

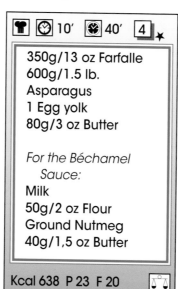

Farfalle with smoked salmon

Served cold, on large platters, this is the ideal pasta dish for buffets, parties, special occasions, or just being together on a summer evening.

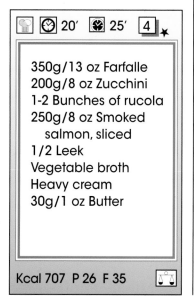

🍴	⏱ 20'	❄ 25'	4 ⭐

350g/13 oz Farfalle
200g/8 oz Zucchini
1-2 Bunches of rucola
250g/8 oz Smoked
   salmon, sliced
1/2 Leek
Vegetable broth
Heavy cream
30g/1 oz Butter

Kcal 707 P 26 F 35 ⚖

Clean the zucchini and cut them into little disks. Clean the leek and slice it thinly. Then, in a saucepan, sauté both vegetables in melted butter, adding a pinch of a salt; moisten with a ladle of broth. Add a dash of ground white pepper, cover and cook slowly over a low flame.

Put the pasta on to cook. Clean the rucola and tear up the leaves.

Cut the salmon into little pieces. When the zucchini are cooked, but still firm, remove the pan from the stove, pour in half a glass of cream, then add the salmon and rucola and mix.

Drain the pasta when it is *al dente*, turn it into the pan and put it back on the stove for an instant over a very low flame, stir once or twice. Serve lukewarm or better yet, cold. Absolutely no cheese on this!

Use a little broth to moisten leftover pasta. Vegetable is better than beef or chicken broth because it is lighter and less flavored. You can either make it yourself, by boiling a carrot, an onion and a stalk of celery in slightly salted water, or using the recipe on page 14 or using any ready-made preparation.

Farfalle Cézanne

Here is a symphony of colors and flavors: the elegance of a still-life evokes the name of the great painter.

Clean the asparagus thoroughly, tie them together in a bunch. Then put them into a large pot where they can stand upright and add enough water to cover the white part of the stalks. Salt slightly. Cook them *al dente*, test with a fork, then drain. Strain the water and set it aside – you will add it to the water for cooking the pasta. Cut off the tough part of the stems, and chop up the rest. Leave a few tips whole, for garnish. While the asparagus are cooking, finely chop the garlic and parsley together and sauté in a skillet with 3-4 tablespoons olive oil. Wash and dry the scampi then toss them into the skillet; let them absorb the flavor over a lively flame and moisten with half a glass of white wine. When the wine has evaporated, add the tomatoes, cut into pieces, lower the flame and cook for 7-8 minutes.

🍳 ⏲ 15'   ✸ 40'   4 ★✦

350g/13 oz Farfalle
16 Fresh scampi
5-600g/1.5 lb. Asparagus
2-3 Ripe tomatoes
1 Clove garlic
Basil
Parsley
Dry white wine
Olive oil

Kcal 491   P 23   F 11   ⚖

Remove the scampi from the pan, but keep them warm. Put the pasta on to cook.
Put the asparagus into the pan, stir

gently over a low flame so they can absorb the flavor.

Drain the farfalle when they are *al dente*, turn them into the pan, add the scampi, toss gently. Use the scampi and basil leaves to decorate the platter. This pasta is delicious served lukewarm, but is also very good cold.

Fusilli smoking

In a bowl, beat the eggs, blend in half a glass of cream and a pinch of salt.
Melt the butter in a skillet and over a low flame, brown the speck (cut into thin strips) along with the chili peppers, if you like. Cook the fusilli *al dente*, drain and turn into the skillet. Remove the chili peppers. (If you did not use the peppers, you can, at this point, add a dash of freshly ground white pepper).
Sprinkle with grated pecorino and cook quickly over a lively flame, moving the mixture so that it does not stick.

🍞 ⏰ 10'   ✿ 20'   4 ★★

350g/13 oz Fusilli
80g/3 oz Speck (1 slice)
2-3 Chili peppers (optional)
2 Egg yolks
Heavy cream
Grated, aged pecorino cheese
30g/1 oz Butter

Kcal 836   P 24   F 50

Pour the contents of the skillet into the bowl with the egg mixture, mix gently and serve hot.

Fusilli with tomatoes and bacon

Wash the tomatoes, remove the seeds and cut them into small chunks. Cut the bacon into cubes and brown in a skillet with a little water. When the bacon is slightly browned, add the tomatoes, a tablespoon of vinegar and a little salt.

🍴 ⏱ 20′	❊ 35′	4	★★

350g/13 oz Fusilli
100 g/4 oz Bacon (1 slice)
4 Ripe tomatoes
Salted capers
Sage
80g/3 oz Black olives
Red wine vinegar
Grated, aged pecorino cheese

Kcal 586 P 17 F 27

Cover and cook over medium heat for 10 minutes. Rinse the capers thoroughly and dry them. Add 50g/2 oz to the sauce, along with 2 torn sage leaves and the pitted, chopped olives. Cook uncovered for another 10 minutes. In the meantime, cook the pasta until it is not quite *al dente*, drain and turn into the skillet, so that it finishes cooking and soaks up the flavors, sprinkle with lots of grated pecorino and toss gently. This dish is meant to be served hot, but it is also good cold.

Fusilli velouté

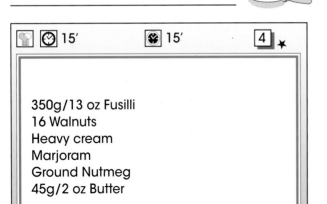

🍳	⏱ 15′	❋ 15′	4 ★

350g/13 oz Fusilli
16 Walnuts
Heavy cream
Marjoram
Ground Nutmeg
45g/2 oz Butter

Kcal 784 P 16 F 48

S hell the walnuts, put 4 aside and chop the rest in the food processor, until they become a paste, add a glass of cream, the leaves from 2 sprigs of marjoram, a pinch of salt and a dash of ground white pepper and nutmeg. The sauce should be velvety smooth.

Cook the fusilli *al dente* then drain. Turn them into a skillet with melted butter, add the nut sauce, and break up the 4 nuts you had set aside; cook over a very low flame, stirring gently.

Remove the skillet from the stove and serve the pasta hot. In our opinion, grated parmesan cheese is not really needed here, but you can use a little.

Eggs and bacon are the basic ingredients for spaghetti alla carbonara. *While the spaghetti is cooking, fry the bacon bits. In a bowl beat 1 egg yolk for each person, grate in enough parmesan to thicken, quickly turn in the drained,* al dente *spaghetti and bacon. Toss so the egg mixture coats the pasta. Season with freshly ground pepper. Using smoked bacon can be considered more or less treason, even though this custom seems to have originated at the end of World War II, when Allied troops supplied the bacon, (and the* penne).

Maccheroncetti with smoked bacon

Clean the onion, chop it finely and sauté it in a skillet in half a glass of broth, but be careful not to let it brown. Add the bacon, cut into bits after about 4-5 minutes, add half a glass of wine and cook over a moderate flame for 10 minutes. Beat the egg yolks in a bowl, add a pinch of salt, black pepper and a big handful of grated parmesan cheese. Set aside.

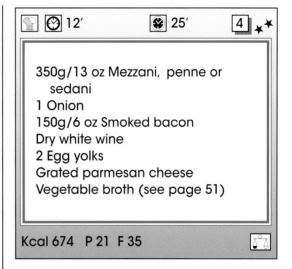

🍳 ⏱ 12'   ❄ 25'   4 ★★

350g/13 oz Mezzani, penne or sedani
1 Onion
150g/6 oz Smoked bacon
Dry white wine
2 Egg yolks
Grated parmesan cheese
Vegetable broth (see page 51)

Kcal 674   P 21   F 35

Cook the pasta and drain it before it reaches the *al dente* point. Turn it into the skillet and cook over a high flame for a few minutes. Pour the contents of the skillet into the bowl and toss so that the pasta is well coated with the egg, add a little more grated parmesan cheese if you like.
Serve hot, it just does not work when lukewarm or cold.

Maccheroni alla Norma

Norma is Vincenzo Bellini's opera heroine. In fact, this dish was created in Catania, the composer's home. The original recipe calls for grated, salted ricotta cheese, but we have adapted it to the continental palate. Were we wrong?

Scald the tomatoes – unless you are using the the canned variety – remove the skins and seeds, and cube them. Rinse and dry the eggplants, cut into them cubes and sauté in a skillet with 5-6 tablespoons olive oil and the peeled clove of garlic. After 8 minutes remove the eggplant cubes using a slotted spoon, drain and put them into a large, warm oven dish. Add the tomatoes to the skillet with a pinch of salt and pepper, cook for about 10 minutes and then add them to the eggplant. Cook the pasta *al dente*, drain, and turn it into the oven dish: add the crumbled ricotta, and the basil leaves, mix well. Another few drops of olive oil will not hurt and serve. It is delicious hot, and just as tasty cold.

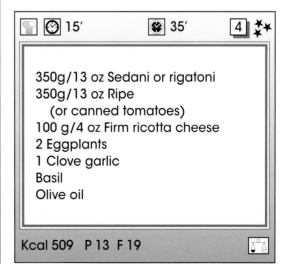

🍳 ⏱ 15'   ❄ 35'   4 ★★

350g/13 oz Sedani or rigatoni
350g/13 oz Ripe
    (or canned tomatoes)
100 g/4 oz Firm ricotta cheese
2 Eggplants
1 Clove garlic
Basil
Olive oil

Kcal 509   P 13   F 19

Mezzani fricassee

C lean the artichokes, remove the stems and tough outer leaves; cut into sections and then into small pieces. Cook in a saucepan with 3-4 tablespoons olive oil, half a ladle of broth and a pinch of salt.

| 🍴 | ⏱ 20' | | � 30' | | 4 | ★★ |

350g/13 oz Mezzani
4 Artichokes
3 Egg yolks
Heavy cream
Grated, aged pecorino cheese
Vegetable broth
Olive oil

Kcal 817   P 24   F 47

Cover and keep the flame low, to cook the artichokes without letting them brown. In the meantime, beat the egg yolks slightly in a bowl, mix in half a glass of cream, a handful of pecorino, a pinch of salt and white pepper. After about 20 minutes, remove the artichokes from the stove – they should be very tender, let them cool a bit and then add them to the egg mixture, mix gently. Set aside. In the meantime, cook the mezzani *al dente*, drain and pour them into the bowl with the eggs and artichokes, mix well and serve.

Mezzani Capodimonte

Cut the olives in half and remove the pits. Wash the tomatoes, cut them in half, remove the seeds and then cut them into chunks.

Grease an oven dish with a little olive oil,

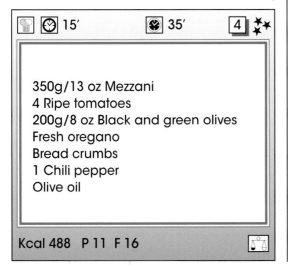

🍳	⏱ 15′		🕐 35′		4	✹✷

350g/13 oz Mezzani
4 Ripe tomatoes
200g/8 oz Black and green olives
Fresh oregano
Bread crumbs
1 Chili pepper
Olive oil

Kcal 488   P 11   F 16

add the tomatoes, olives and the crushed chili pepper.

Cook the mezzani, drain them just before they reach the *al dente* point and turn them into the oven dish.

Dress the pasta with a squiggle of olive oil, a pinch of oregano and mix well so that all the flavors blend thoroughly.

Sprinkle the top with breadcrumbs and bake at 200°C (400°F) for 10 minutes.

Serve hot, the flavor is as delicate and fresh as the porcelain they are named after.

Cheese is not recommended, in fact it is much better to do without it.

Mezzani alla Luciana

This recipe requires some time: the octopus will only become tender if you let it cool in the cooking water, and that may take an hour or more.

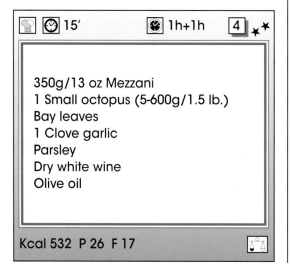

🗓 ⏱ 15′   ❀ 1h+1h   4 ★★

350g/13 oz Mezzani
1 Small octopus (5-600g/1.5 lb.)
Bay leaves
1 Clove garlic
Parsley
Dry white wine
Olive oil

Kcal 532 P 26 F 17

The octopus has to be well cleaned – usually the more complicated tasks are done by the fish vendor.
Put the octopus into a pot of cold water with 2 bay leaves. Cover, bring to the boil and then lower the flame.
The octopus should be done in one hour. Let it cool in the cooking water, then drain it and cut it into pieces. Gently sauté a mixture of chopped garlic and parsley in a skillet with 3-4 tablespoons olive oil; add the octopus pieces, a pinch of salt, pepper and half a glass of white wine, cook over a low flame so that most of the liquid absorbs.
In the meantime, cook the mezzani, drain just before they are *al dente*, and turn them into the skillet, cook for 2 minutes stirring to blend. Garnish the plates with parsley leaves – and do not add cheese.

Mezzani au gratin

To prepare the béchamel sauce, slowly melt the butter in a saucepan over a low flame; when it is completely melted add the flour, one spoonful at a time, stirring constantly – in the same direction – with a wooden spoon so that no lumps form. When the mixture is an even golden-brown, add the milk, a little at a time, and keep on stirring; add pinch of salt, white pepper and ground nutmeg. Blend over a very low flame, then remove from the stove and set aside.
Cook the mezzani and drain before they are *al dente*.
Place the pasta in a buttered oven dish and dress with about three quarters of the

béchamel, lots of grated parmesan cheese and dot with butter. Spread the rest of the béchamel over the top and sprinkle with parmesan cheese. Bake at 180°C/350°F for about 10 minutes.

🗓 ⏱ 5′   ❀ 35′   4 ★

350g/13 oz Mezzani
Breadcrumbs
Grated parmesan cheese
60g/2 oz Butter

For the béchamel sauce:
40g/1.5 oz Butter
Milk
50g/2 oz Flour
Ground nutmeg

Kcal 697   P 20 F 30

This delicious "seafood" mezzani (actually, you can use thick spaghetti instead of mezzani) can also be made using moscardini instead of octopus. Moscardini are easier to clean (you should still let the fish vendor do it anyway) and faster to cook. The Italian name "moscardino" comes from the fact that it is a totally different, not merely miniature, variety of octopus with a distinct musky fragrance.

Orecchiette with broccoli

15'+30'	40'	4	★ ★

250g/8 oz Orecchiette
800g/28 oz Broccoli
2 Cloves garlic
Fresh chili peppers
2 Anchovies
3 Ripe tomatoes
Basil
Olive oil

Kcal 417 P 18 F 12

Clean the broccoli and cook in slightly salted water, until done, but firm. Drain and put the water aside for cooking the pasta. Chop the broccoli and eliminate as much of the stems as possible. In a skillet sauté a clove of garlic until golden in 3-4 tablespoons olive oil then remove it: add the broccoli, 2 chopped chili peppers and a pinch of salt; simmer for 5-6 minutes. In the meantime, cook the orecchiette *al dente*. Drain and turn into the skillet with the broccoli, cook over a high flame, stirring with wooden spoon for 1 minute. Turn off the flame and add the tomatoes, mix well to blend. Serve hot. Cheese is not really appropriate here, but, if you must...use pecorino.

Clean and filet the anchovies. Scald the tomatoes, remove the skin and seeds. Put them in a bowl together with the finely chopped garlic, basil leaves and the anchovies broken into little pieces. Set aside for a half hour.

The real orecchiette *from the Puglia region of Italy that are made with semolina and water "yield" more than other types of pasta, that is why we recommend using less.*

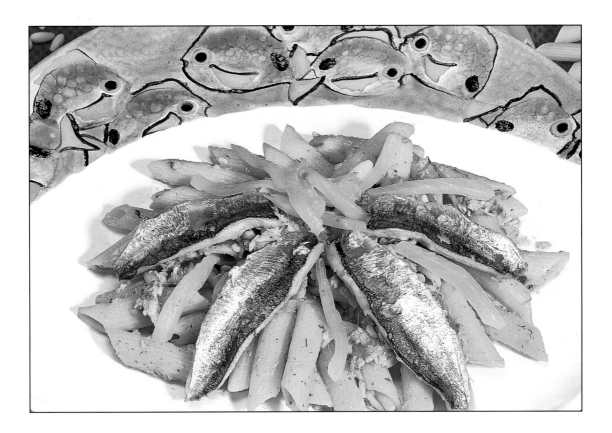

Pasta with sardines

Soak the raisins. Filet the anchovies and half the sardines. Open the other half, bone and cut off the heads without filleting. Chop the onion and sauté it in a saucepan with 4-5 tablespoons olive oil, add the sardine and anchovy filets, cooking until they soften and practically dissolve. Drain and squeeze out the raisins, add them to the fish along with salt, the wild fennel, saffron and chili pepper, continue cooking, but do not let the mixture become dry. Put up water with a little coarse salt and a sprig of wild fennel: cook the pasta *al dente*. In the meantime, slightly brown the other sardines in a skillet with 3-4 tablespoons olive oil, garlic and wild fennel. Drain the pasta, turn it into an oven dish, dress with the fish and arrange the whole sardines on top; sprinkle with breadcrumbs and bake at 160°C (320°F) for 10 minutes.

Wild fennel is an essential ingredient in this Sicilian recipe, and is available dried. If you cannot find it in your store, use dill.

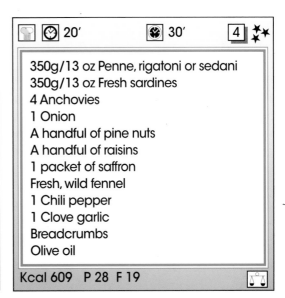

🕒 20′   ❋ 30′   4 ✹✹

350g/13 oz Penne, rigatoni or sedani
350g/13 oz Fresh sardines
4 Anchovies
1 Onion
A handful of pine nuts
A handful of raisins
1 packet of saffron
Fresh, wild fennel
1 Chili pepper
1 Clove garlic
Breadcrumbs
Olive oil

Kcal 609   P 28   F 19

Penne Barcarola

If you use frozen shrimp, leave enough time for them to defrost.

Rinse the anchovies under running water and fillet them. Wash the tomatoes, remove the seeds and cut them into cubes, wash the rucola and tear the leaves with your hands.

Finely chop together the garlic, parsley and one chili pepper, sauté in a skillet with 4 tablespoons olive oil. Add the anchovies and cook over a very low flame until they dissolve (if you prefer, you can use an equivalent amount of anchovy paste), add the tomatoes and cook slowly for 15 minutes more.

Cook the pasta and drain it just before it reaches the *al dente* point. Turn the pasta into the skillet, add the shrimp, cook and stir for a minute or two. Cheese is definitely not appropriate.

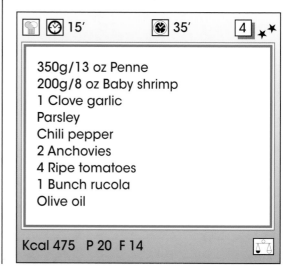

🍮	⏱ 15′		❀ 35′		4	★★

350g/13 oz Penne
200g/8 oz Baby shrimp
1 Clove garlic
Parsley
Chili pepper
2 Anchovies
4 Ripe tomatoes
1 Bunch rucola
Olive oil

Kcal 475 P 20 F 14

Penne with baby octopus

Wash the tomatoes, remove the seeds and cut them into cubes. Clean and wash the octopus (actually, let your fish vendor do it, it is neither simple nor pleasant!), then cut it up into little pieces.

Sauté the crushed garlic and chopped parsley in a saucepan with 4 tablespoons olive oil.

Add the octopus and cook over a low flame for 10 minutes. Pour half a glass of white wine over it and when the wine has evaporated add the tomatoes, a pinch of salt and the chili pepper in pieces.

Cover and cook over a medium flame for 50 minutes, add a little broth now and then as needed.

Cook the pasta and drain it just before it reaches the *al dente* point. Turn the pasta into the pan, and cook over a high flame for 2-3 minutes, garnish with finely chopped parsley and serve.

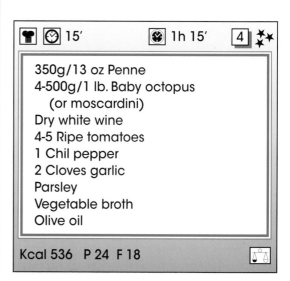

🍴	⏱ 15′		❀ 1h 15′		4	★★★

350g/13 oz Penne
4-500g/1 lb. Baby octopus
    (or moscardini)
Dry white wine
4-5 Ripe tomatoes
1 Chil pepper
2 Cloves garlic
Parsley
Vegetable broth
Olive oil

Kcal 536 P 24 F 18

Are you interested in a tasty variation of Penne Barcarola? *Make pesto, following the instructions on page 34. In a skillet, gently sauté a mixture of chopped parsley, garlic and chili pepper with 4-5 tablespoons olive oil; add 500g/1 lb. clams (preferably small ones) raise the heat so* they open. Scald baby shrimp and set them aside. Cook the penne al dente *dress with a generous amount of* pesto *and mix in the clams and a tablespoon of their cooking liquid. Arrange on individual plates and decorate with the baby shrimp, and a sprig of parsley.*

Pennette with rabbit

Pasta dressed with rabbit sauce is so good that it a traditional recipe is warranted, and this one is very excellent. It is a traditional dish from Sardinia, flavored with myrtle.

Clean the rabbit, cut it into pieces as small as possible and remove the bigger bones. Brown it in a skillet with 4-5 tablespoons olive oil, salt and pepper, and a few sage, myrtle and rosemary leaves. Moisten with a glass of white wine and cook for 15 minutes over a medium flame, add broth as necessary if it tends to dry. In the meantime, cook the pasta and drain it just before it reaches the *al dente* point. Turn it into the skillet and cook over a high flame for a few minutes. Serve piping hot, garnished with basil leaves and rosemary.

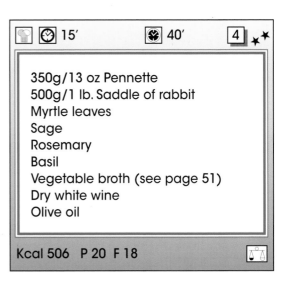

🕐 15'   ❀ 40'   4 ★★

350g/13 oz Pennette
500g/1 lb. Saddle of rabbit
Myrtle leaves
Sage
Rosemary
Basil
Vegetable broth (see page 51)
Dry white wine
Olive oil

Kcal 506   P 20   F 18

Poor man's pennette

Clean the onions, if you are using the white rather than the red variety, increase the amount to 5-6 – they are more delicately flavored, and cut them into rings.

Sauté gently in a skillet with 4 tablespoons olive oil, a pinch of salt, and half a glass of vegetable broth. Cover the skillet so that the onions cook over a very low flame for about 30 minutes;, they should become tender without browning or burning.

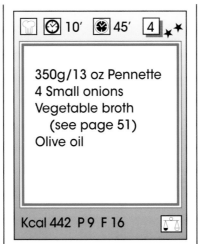

🕐 10' ⏱ 45' 4 ★✦

350g/13 oz Pennette
4 Small onions
Vegetable broth
   (see page 51)
Olive oil

Kcal 442 P 9 F 16

Cook the pasta drain while still quite firm and turn it into the skillet with the onions, mix carefully.

Just before serving, add a dash of freshly ground white pepper, whether or not to use cheese is up to you!

Sedani with fennel and tomatoes

🗑 ⏱ 10'   ❀ 45'   4 ★★

350g/13 oz Sedani
400g/14 oz Ripe tomatoes
1 Small fennel (or half a large one)
Chili peppers
Fresh oregano
Vegetable broth (see page 51)
Grated parmesan cheese
Olive oil

Kcal 466   P 14   F 14

Heat 4 tablespoons olive oil in a small skillet, add 2-3 chili peppers and sauté them gently until softened, remove the peppers and let the oil cool.

Scald the tomatoes in boiling water, peel them, remove the seeds and cut them into strips.

Clean the fennel and slice it, then cut the slices in half. Cook the fennel in a saucepan with a ladle of broth, the flavored oil and a pinch of salt.

Cover, and cook slowly for 20 minutes. Turn off the flame, remove the cover and dust with fresh oregano.

In the meantime cook the pasta *al dente*, and drain. Dress it with the sauce, a generous sprinkling of grated parmesan cheese and a few oregano leaves for trim.

Rigatoni Marinella

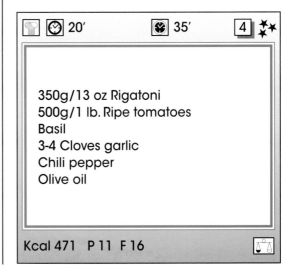

Wash the basil, dry the leaves and remove the stems. Tear up the leaves by hand (an old folk custom decrees that basil should never touch metal!). Scald the tomatoes in boiling water, remove the skins and seeds, then cut them into cubes.

Sauté one clove of garlic and a chili pepper in a skillet with 4-5 tablespoons olive oil. As soon as the garlic starts to brown, remove both and add the tomatoes, the rest of the garlic and a pinch of salt. Cover and cook slowly for 20 minutes.

In the meantime, cook the rigatoni and drain just before they reach the *al dente* point. Turn the pasta into the skillet and cook over a high flame for a couple of minutes.

Remove the garlic and serve, using fresh basil leaves as garnish. A squiggle of olive oil will not hurt either, but cheese is not really advisable unless it is exquisite Romano or Sienese pecorino and then, just a little.

🍳 ⏰ 20'	⏱ 35'	4 ✷✷✷

350g/13 oz Rigatoni
500g/1 lb. Ripe tomatoes
Basil
3-4 Cloves garlic
Chili pepper
Olive oil

Kcal 471　P 11　F 16

Rigatoni al fresco

Break the egg into a bowl, add the yolk, a bit of mustard and a pinch of salt. Add a drop of oil, stirring constantly, and always in the same direction, with a wooden spoon. As the mixture thickens, add the oil drop by drop (in all it should be 1 dl/ 1/2 cup), stir in the juice of half a lemon. Refrigerate the mayonnaise.

Wash and slice the pepper and tomatoes, put them under the broiler for 10 minutes; remove the skins, cool and cut into strips.

Cook the rigatoni *al dente*, drain and cool in a bowl of cold water. Turn the pasta into a bowl and dress with the mayonnaise and 2 tablespoons olive oil. Add the tomatoes and peppers, mix, and refrigerate for 30 minutes. Fillet the anchovies, rinse a handful of capers and pat them dry with a paper towel. Clean and chop the parsley. Cut the olives in half.

Add the broken up anchovies, capers, parsley and olives to the pasta, mix well, garnish with fresh basil leaves and serve.

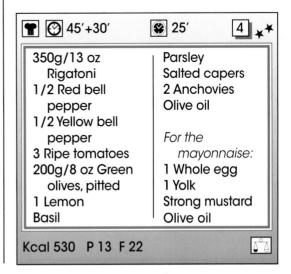

🍴 🕐 45'+30'	❀ 25'	4 ⭐
350g/13 oz Rigatoni	Parsley	
1/2 Red bell pepper	Salted capers	
1/2 Yellow bell pepper	2 Anchovies	
3 Ripe tomatoes	Olive oil	
200g/8 oz Green olives, pitted	*For the mayonnaise:*	
1 Lemon	1 Whole egg	
Basil	1 Yolk	
	Strong mustard	
	Olive oil	

Kcal 530   P 13   F 22

Sedani with beans (or all'uccelletto)

"Fagioli all'uccelletto" is a typical Tuscan dish. White beans are recooked with tomato sauce, garlic and sage. It is delicious, but who would have ever thought of using those beans to dress pasta? It is a hearty dish and makes a full meal by itself. If you use dried beans, you must soak them for a couple of hours beforehand.

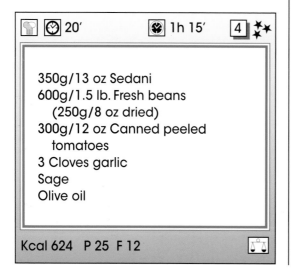

🍳 ⏰ 20'   ❀ 1h 15'   4 ✹✹

350g/13 oz Sedani
600g/1.5 lb. Fresh beans
   (250g/8 oz dried)
300g/12 oz Canned peeled
   tomatoes
3 Cloves garlic
Sage
Olive oil

Kcal 624   P 25   F 12

Shell the beans and put them in a pot of cold water. Cover and slowly bring to the boil, add a pinch of salt and continue cooking slowly for about 30 minutes. Wash the tomatoes, remove the seeds and cut them into pieces. Sauté a clove of garlic and 2-3 sage leaves in a skillet with 3-4 tablespoons olive oil. Add the tomatoes, a pinch of salt, peeper and cook slowly for about 20 minutes. Drain the beans and add them to the tomatoes along with the rest of the garlic, and a few more sage leaves. Mix and cook over a low flame for another 15 minutes. Cook the rigatoni and drain just before they are *al dente*. Turn the pasta into the skillet, mix well and serve – not too hot. And, don't even consider adding cheese!

Sedani di Vinicio

Clean and thoroughly wash the spinach. Scald it in boiling water with a pinch of salt. Drain, squeeze out the water and chop coarsely. Clean the peppers, open them remove the seeds and white membrane and cut them into narrow strips.

Clean the onion and chop it finely with the garlic and a few basil leaves: sauté the mixture in a skillet with 4-5 tablespoons olive oil.

Add the peppers, a couple of chili peppers and cook over a high flame for 4-5 minutes.

Add the spinach and 2 glasses of wine, lower the flame and cook for about 15 minutes.

Cook the pasta and drain it just before it is *al dente*. Turn it into the skillet and mix well.

Turn off the flame and let it cool to lukewarm, serve with a squiggle of extra virgin olive oil. Cheese? Pecorino or nothing.

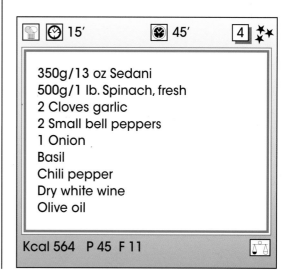

🕒 15'   ✤ 45'   4 ✦✦

350g/13 oz Sedani
500g/1 lb. Spinach, fresh
2 Cloves garlic
2 Small bell peppers
1 Onion
Basil
Chili pepper
Dry white wine
Olive oil

Kcal 564 P 45 F 11

Sweet sedani

Is this is a first course or a dessert? The choice is up to you, but the fact remains that this is one of the most original solutions for tarting or ending a meal – especially on a special occasion.

Cook the pasta with just the tiniest pinch of salt (strange as it may seem a little salt will not alter the flavor at all).
While the pasta is cooking, use a fork to blend the ricotta with a tablespoon of sugar and a tablespoon of the boiling water from the pasta.

Drain the sedani *al dente*, turn it into the bowl with the ricotta and sprinkle

🍴 ⏲ 10′ ⏰ 10′ 4 ★

350g/13 oz Sedani
200g/8 oz Ricotta
   cheese
Sugar
Powdered cinnamon

Kcal 376 P 17 F 4 ⚖

with a little cinnamon. This is wonderful served hot, to add a festive touch – top it with a handful of presoaked, squeezed out raisins. Or, after you add the raisins you can turn it into a buttered oven dish and bake for 10 minutes at 180 °C/350 °F.

Sedani with shrimp and mushrooms

If you use frozen shrimp, be sure to leave enough time for them to thaw. Clean and wash the mushrooms; pat them dry and cut them into pieces. Sauté them in a skillet with 2-3 tablespoons olive oil, a dash of salt and white pepper.

After 5 minutes add a glass of cream, a pinch of ground nutmeg and chopped parsley. Cook for 5-6 minutes over a very low flame.

Cook the pasta and drain it right before it reaches the *al dente* point, turn it into the skillet. Add the shrimp and mix so that the sauce covers the pasta like a velvety veil. Serve lukewarm.

If you want to add a super touch of class, cover the top with thinly sliced white truffle.

15' 20' 4 ★

350g/13 oz Sedani
200g/8 oz Mushrooms
200g/8 oz Baby shrimp
Heavy cream
Grated parmesan cheese
Parsley
Ground nutmeg
Olive oil

Kcal 742 P 24 F 39

Tortiglioni Piedigrotta

Scald the tomatoes and peel them; remove the seeds and cut them into cubes. Cut the olives in half and pit them. Cook the tortiglioni and drain when they are four fifths done. Turn the pasta into an oven dish and dress with 2 tablespoons olive oil.

Combine the tomatoes, the mozzarella cut into cubes, the olives, a pinch of salt and a few oregano leaves.

Put under the broiler at 200°C (400°F) for 8-10 minutes, or until the mozzarella is melted. Serve piping hot.

🕙 10'   ✹ 30'   4 ✯✯

350g/13 oz Tortiglioni
4-5 Ripe tomatoes
1 Mozzarella
16 Black olives
Fresh oregano
Olive oil

Kcal 479   P 11   F 17

Tortiglioni with zucchini

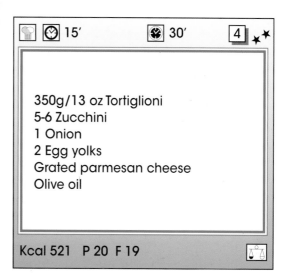

This is very similar to "carbonara", except that instead of bacon – to follow the advice of the wizard of Italian cooking, Artusi – it is made with zucchini for "delicate stomachs". How does it taste? Well, try it and you will see.

Clean the zucchini; pat them dry and cut them into 6 mm (1/4 inch) thick disks. Clean the onion, slice it thinly and sauté it in a skillet with 4-5 tablespoons olive oil. Add the zucchini, spreading them out so they overlap as little as possible, add salt and pepper. Turn the zucchini so that they become a nice golden brown on both sides.

Beat the egg yolks in a bowl and sprinkle generously with grated parmesan cheese and a dash of black pepper. Cook the tortiglioni *al dente*, drain. Turn the pasta into the bowl, add the zucchini and mix well. Serve immediately.

🍴 ⏲ 15′	✿ 30′	4 ★✦

350g/13 oz Tortiglioni
5-6 Zucchini
1 Onion
2 Egg yolks
Grated parmesan cheese
Olive oil

Kcal 521   P 20   F 19

Tortiglioni with clams

If you buy the clams the night before you use them, or early in the morning, to keep them fresh wrap them in a wet dish towel and put them in the coldest part of your refrigerator, but not the freezer.

The best way to eliminate the sand in the clams is to soak them in slightly salted water. Place a dish upside down in the bottom of the bowl with the salted water. As if by magic, the sand from the clams will collect under the dish. Change the water 2 or 3 times until there is no trace of sand. Since most clams come from "farms", the sand is finer than normal sea sand and you may need to change the water more than 3 times, but it is well worth the effort. Discard the dead clams, the ones that don't open partly in the clean water, and obviously the little scoundrels that don't open when heated.

🍴	⏱ 10'+6-7h	❀ 20'	4	✦✦

350g/13 oz Whole wheat tortiglioni
1kg/2 lb. Clams
1 Clove garlic
2 Green onions
Dry white wine
Olive oil

Kcal 486 P 15 F 17

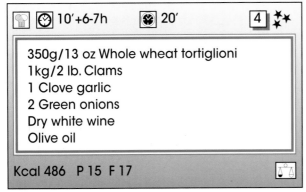

Clean and slice the onions. Put the rinsed clams into a skillet with a little olive oil and the garlic. Heat over a high flame so they open, douse with half a glass of white wine and cook until the wine evaporates.

Turn off the flame, remove the clams (set them aside and keep them hot) and the garlic.

You may have to strain the liquid through cheesecloth if the clams were not perfectly rinsed.

Cook the pasta and drain just before they reach the *al dente* point, put it into the skillet with the liquid from the clams and cook over a high flame for a few minutes. Turn off the flame, add the sliced onions and mix. Add the clams in their open shells and serve. This is a fragrant and original dish, but remember – no cheese – ever!

FRESH AND FILLED
PASTA

Agnolini in broth

Agnolini, *are very similar to cappelletti and are typical of the area around Mantua. This is the traditional recipe, made easier by the fact that now there are blenders and pasta machines.*

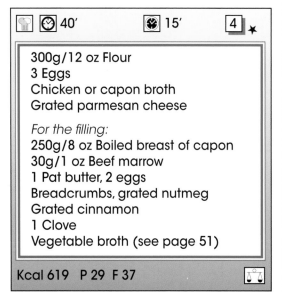

| 🍳 | ⏰ 40′ | | ✿ 15′ | | 4 ★ |

300g/12 oz Flour
3 Eggs
Chicken or capon broth
Grated parmesan cheese

For the filling:
250g/8 oz Boiled breast of capon
30g/1 oz Beef marrow
1 Pat butter, 2 eggs
Breadcrumbs, grated nutmeg
Grated cinnamon
1 Clove
Vegetable broth (see page 51)

Kcal 619   P 29   F 37

Mound the flour on your work table, make a well in the middle and break the eggs into it, add a pinch of salt and knead (see pictures on the next page). Melt the butter in a skillet, add the marrow and cook slowly until it dissolves.

Chop the capon breast in the blender, add the marrow, 2 eggs, grated parmesan cheese, half a glass of broth, breadcrumbs, salt and pepper, the clove, a pinch each of ground nutmeg and cinnamon and blend at low speed until evenly mixed and firm. Roll out the dough thinly and use a glass or round cookie cutter to cut 5 cm (2 inch) diameter circles.

Place a teaspoon of filling in the middle of each, fold in half and press the edges to seal; then fold in half again and press to seal.

Cook the agnolini in chicken or capon broth and serve with grated parmesan cheese.

Making egg pasta

1 The ingredients for any type of fresh pasta are always the same (sometimes you may have to add a little water or oil according to the specific recipes): 100 g/4 oz durum wheat flour per person for cut pasta (tagliatelle, fettuccini, etc.) and about 75g/3 oz for filled pasta, 1 egg for each 100 g/4 oz flour, and a pinch of salt. Mound the flour on the work table – marble is the best – and the place you work should be dry.

2 Flour your hands (this keeps the dough from sticking to your fingers) and knead the flour and eggs, working from the outside towards the middle. Work slowly but firmly until the dough is evenly blended and elastic.
According to the elasticity, or how soft the dough is supposed to be you may add a little oil or water (usually 2 tablespoons unless otherwise specified).

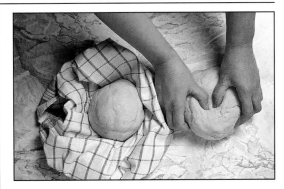

3 Shape the dough into a ball (if you are working with a large quantity, make two balls), wrap in a clean cloth or plastic wrap and put aside in a cool, dry place for a half hour. Shape the dough into a loaf.

4 Lightly flour the work table and rolling pin (unless, of course, you are using a pasta machine). Cut each loaf into 15 mm (1 1/2 inch) thick slices – this makes it easier to work with the pasta. Roll out the dough to the desired thickness and then cut to shape (see page 89).

Agnolotti in meat sauce

🍳 ⏱ 30′	❄ 2h 15′	4 ✪✪	Kcal 670 P 28 F 42	⚖

300g/12oz Flour 3 Eggs Olive oil	*For the filling:* 300g/12 oz Beef rump 60g/2 oz Lean bacon 3 Slices salami – without garlic Grated parmesan cheese	1 onion 1 Egg Ground nutmeg Dry white wine 60g/2 oz Butter

Agnolotti *are a specialty of the Piemonte region; the filling is usually made with a mixture of fresh and processed meats.*

Finely chop the onion and sauté it in a saucepan in half the melted butter. Add the beef, salt and pepper and brown slowly; cover with wine, put on the lid and cook over a very low flame for about 2 hours, adding a little more wine now and then as needed. Melt the rest of the butter in a skillet, and the cut up bacon and salami. In the blender, finely chop the beef, bacon and salami, add 1 egg, a dash of nutmeg and a handful of grated parmesan cheese blend at low speed.

Prepare the pasta (see page 85) with 2 tablespoons olive oil.

Roll out the dough thinly into wide strips; use a pasta cutter to make rectangles 4 x 8 cm (2 x 3 1/2 inches) (steps 3 and 4 of the instructions on page 122). Place two, nut-size dabs of the meat mixture on each, fold over, press to seal the edges and then cut each one in half using the cutter. Use up all the pasta and filling. Sprinkle the agnolotti lightly with flour and cook in boiling water. Dress with meat sauce and serve.

Meat sauce: 250g/8 oz chopped beef; 1 carrot; 1 onion, 1 stalk celery; half a glass of red wine; 200g/8 oz crushed, peeled canned tomatoes (or tomato purée) and good olive oil. Follow the step-by-step instructions:

1 Clean and chop the vegetables. Slowly sauté in a saucepan with 3-4 tablespoons olive oil. Add the meat and brown in slowly.

2 Pour in the wine and let it evaporate over a medium flame. Salt and pepper to taste before you add the tomatoes. This way the meat will get flavor from its own juices that are drawn out by the salt.

3 Add the tomatoes, - or the purée, stir and cook over a moderate flame for a few minutes. Lower the flame and cover the saucepan.

4 Cook covered for about 1 one hour. If necessary add a little broth to keep it from sticking. Uncover, and cook until it thickens, the sauce should not be runny.

Bavette timbale

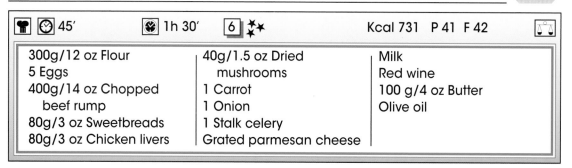

🍴 ⏱ 45′	❀ 1h 30′	6 ✬✬	Kcal 731 P 41 F 42	⚖

300g/12 oz Flour	40g/1.5 oz Dried	Milk
5 Eggs	mushrooms	Red wine
400g/14 oz Chopped	1 Carrot	100 g/4 oz Butter
beef rump	1 Onion	Olive oil
80g/3 oz Sweetbreads	1 Stalk celery	
80g/3 oz Chicken livers	Grated parmesan cheese	

Actually the word bavette is a type of dry pasta, but we use it here for the finest, thinnest imaginable tagliatelle. You can make the timbale using the dry bavette too, but there is no comparison with the pasta you make yourself...is there? (see the instructions on the next page).

Prepare the pasta dough (page 85) with the flour and 3 eggs. While the dough is resting, soak the mushrooms, clean the vegetables and chop them finely. Sauté half the vegetables in a small saucepan with 3 tablespoons olive oil: add half the chopped beef to brown, with a few tablespoons of wine and cook slowly for 20 minutes, add a little water now and then if needed; salt and pepper to taste. Scald the sweetbreads in boiling water and remove the skins.

Clean the chicken livers, rinse them under cold running water and dry. Break the other eggs into a bowl, mix with a handful of grated parmesan cheese,

60g/2 oz melted butter and a pinch of salt; moisten with a glass of milk, add the browned chopped beef and set aside. Drain the mushrooms, squeeze out the excess water and chop them finely. In a small skillet, sauté the other half of the chopped vegetables in a pat of butter, add the mushrooms, and the rest of the chopped meat; brown slowly. Cut up the sweetbreads, chop the chicken livers and add them to the skillet, douse with half a glass of wine and cook slowly for about 20 minutes; salt and pepper to taste. Roll out the dough – not too thinly – and cut bavette (see below). Cook the bavette *al dente* drain and turn them into the bowl with the chopped meat and egg mixture, blend. Place in a well-buttered tube pan and bake at 160-180°C 320°-350°F for 15 minutes. Turn out onto a serving platter and fill the center hole with the tasty meat filling.

Tagliatelle, taglierini & c.

1 Shape the dough into loaves and slice (see page 85). On a floured work table, roll each slice out to a sheet of 12x45 cm (5 x 18 inches). Roll the edges of each slide towards the middle – like a parchment scroll.

3 If you cut narrower strips (from 1 cm to 5 mm – that is 1/2 to 1 or 2 inch) you will be making "*tagliatelle*" to serve with sauce or butter, "*taglierini*" (to cook in broth), "*bavette*", etc.

2 Cut each roll into strip of the desired size. The one shown here (2-3 cm/1-1 1/2 inches) is for "*strisce*" or "*pappardelle*". If you want scalloped edges, use the pasta cutter wheel.

4 By cutting tiny strips (3-4 mm – less than 1/2 inch) you will be making "*quadrucci*" or other small pasta for cooking and eating in broth. Gather up the scraps, knead them together, roll out and cut until you have used all the dough.

Cannelloni with mushrooms

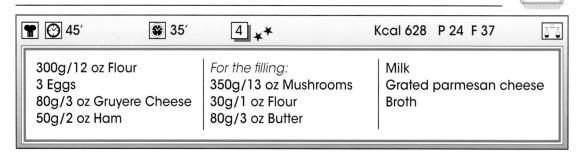

🍴 ⏱ 45′	❄ 35′	4 ★✦	Kcal 628 P 24 F 37	⚖

300g/12 oz Flour	*For the filling:*	Milk
3 Eggs	350g/13 oz Mushrooms	Grated parmesan cheese
80g/3 oz Gruyere Cheese	30g/1 oz Flour	Broth
50g/2 oz Ham	80g/3 oz Butter	

1 Prepare the dough (see page 85) and set it aside to rest. Make a thick béchamel sauce: melt 50g/2 oz butter, add 3 tablespoons flour and gradually add 1 cup milk (and a pinch of salt). Clean the mushrooms and slice thinly. Sauté in a skillet in the rest of the melted butter.

3 Place the filling on the noodles and roll them up – now they are really cannelloni! Arrange them in a buttered oven dish.

2 Roll out the dough and cut it into 10 x 18 cm (4 x 7 inches) rectangles. Cook the noodles *al dente* drain and dry on a clean dish cloth. In a bowl combine two thirds of the béchamel with the sautéed mushrooms (set aside a couple of tablespoons of the mushrooms for garnish), 3 tablespoons grated parmesan cheese, salt and half a glass of broth.

4 Spread the rest of the béchamel over the top. Arrange slices of ham and strips of cheese in a lattice and sprinkle with grated parmesan cheese. Bake at 180°C (350°F) for 15 minutes, or until the cheese topping melts. Remove, let cool just a bit and scatter the remaining mushrooms over the top.

Sicilian cannelloni

🍴 ⏱ 45′	⏲ 35′	4 ✵✶	Kcal 1005 P 31 F 73	⚖

300g/12 oz Flour 3 Eggs *For the filling* 300g/12 oz Ricotta cheese	1 Glass cream 50g/2 oz Pine nuts 50g/2 oz Raisins 1 Onion Chili pepper 150g/6 oz Ham	100 g/4 oz Pecorino cheese Dry Marsala Tomato sauce Olive oil

1 Prepare the dough (see page 85) and set it aside to rest. Prepare all the ingredients for the filling: first of all soak the raisins in lukewarm water; dice the ham. Finely chop the onion and sauté it in a saucepan with 3-4 tablespoons olive oil.

3 Roll out the dough and cut it into 10 x 18 cm (4 x 7 inches) rectangles. Cook the noodles *al dente* drain and dry on a clean dish cloth, be sure that they do not overlap! Place the filling on the noodles and roll them up and arrange them in a buttered oven dish.

2 Combine the ricotta with the cream and add it to the onion, along with the pine nuts, the squeezed out raisins, a dash of salt and chili pepper. Stir, add the Marsala and let it blend over a low flame for a minutes. Add the diced ham.

4 Make two layers of cannelloni and spread tomato sauce over it. Sprinkle with 2 handfuls of grated pecorino, and some caraway seeds (if you like the flavor). Bake at 200°C (400°F) for 20 minutes.

Super cannelloni

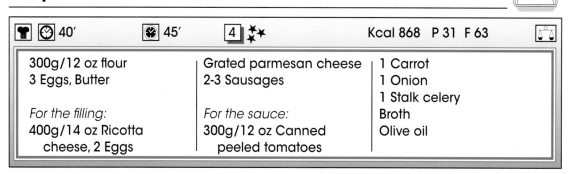

🍴 ⏰ 40′	🕐 45′	4 ✹✦	Kcal 868 P 31 F 63	⚖

300g/12 oz flour
3 Eggs, Butter
 	
For the filling:
400g/14 oz Ricotta
  cheese, 2 Eggs
	Grated parmesan cheese
	2-3 Sausages
	
	For the sauce:
	300g/12 oz Canned
	  peeled tomatoes
		1 Carrot
		1 Onion
		1 Stalk celery
		Broth
		Olive oil		

1 Prepare the dough (see page 85) and set aside to rest. In a bowl, combine the ricotta, a dash of salt, 3-4 tablespoons grated parmesan cheese and 2 slightly beaten eggs, blend with a fork.

2 Puncture the sausages with a fork and brown them in a skillet with a little water. Skin and crumble the sausages. Clean and chop the vegetables and sauté in a skillet with 3-4 tablespoons olive oil, add the tomatoes, a little salt and cook for 20 minutes over a low flame adding a little water now then as needed.

3 Add the crumbled sausages to the ricotta mixture. Roll out the dough and cut it into 10 x 18 cm (4 x 7 inches) rectangles. Cook the noodles *al dente* drain and dry on a clean dish cloth, be sure that they do not overlap!

4 Place the filling on the noodles and roll up the cannelloni. Arrange them, in a single layer, in a buttered oven dish and bake at 200°C (400)°F for 10 minutes. Remove from the oven and sprinkle with the tomato sauce, put back into the oven for 5 minutes more. Sprinkle with grated parmesan cheese and serve.

Nastrini alla pizzaiola

Prepare the dough as shown on page 85 and cut the nastrini – which means ribbons – following the instructions on page 89. Cook until the noodles are *al dente* drain and dress with 60g/2 oz

butter and two handfuls of grated parmesan cheese.

Butter an oven dish and arrange the noodles, moisten with a glass of cream. Place mozzarella slices on top and cover with the tomato sauce and sprinkle with grated parmesan cheese. Bake at 180°-200°C (350°-400°F) until the mozzarella starts to melt. Remove from the oven and serve immediately.

If you want to enhance the resemblance to pizza, do not use parmesan, rather add oregano, capers and anchovy slices (or, skip the anchovies if you prefer a "pizza Margherita") before you put it in the oven, and garnish with a few basil leaves just before serving.

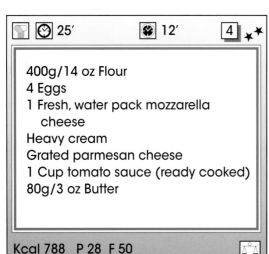

🍳 ⏰ 25′	❀ 12′	4 ★★

400g/14 oz Flour
4 Eggs
1 Fresh, water pack mozzarella cheese
Heavy cream
Grated parmesan cheese
1 Cup tomato sauce (ready cooked)
80g/3 oz Butter

Kcal 788   P 28   F 50

Gnocchetti with codfish

Boil the potatoes in the jackets, peel and cut into chunks. Chop 1 shallot and sauté in a saucepan with 1 clove garlic and 2-3 tablespoons olive oil; add the codfish fillets, douse with half a glass white wine, salt and pepper. Cook for 5 minutes over a high flame. Put the fish into the blender and combine with the potatoes. Blend the fish and potatoes with 120g/5 oz flour, chopped parsley, the egg, salt and pepper. Shape the mixture into tangerine-size balls and set aside for 30 minutes. Chop the garlic and shallot together finely and sauté in a skillet, along with the sage and rosemary in 3 tablespoons olive oil. Add the anchovies and tomatoes and simmer over a low flame for 5 minutes. Turn off the flame and pour in a cup of cream add salt and keep warm. Now, take the little balls and roll them into sticks, cut pieces about 2-3 cm (1 inch) long. Cook the gnocchi in salted water, when they float up to the top it means that they are done; drain and put them into a serving bowl, dress with the sauce, toss gently, cover and let them absorb the flavor for a few minutes before serving. Garnish the plates with sprigs of rosemary.

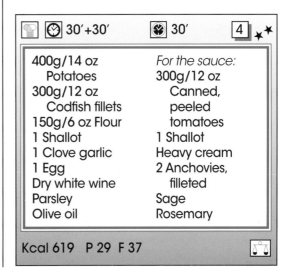

🍞 ⏱ 30'+30'	❀ 30'	4 ★✦

400g/14 oz Potatoes	*For the sauce:*
300g/12 oz Codfish fillets	300g/12 oz Canned, peeled tomatoes
150g/6 oz Flour	1 Shallot
1 Shallot	Heavy cream
1 Clove garlic	2 Anchovies, filleted
1 Egg	Sage
Dry white wine	Rosemary
Parsley	
Olive oil	

Kcal 619   P 29   F 37

Gnocchi with nettles

Scald the nettle leaves in salted water, drain and squeeze out the excess water. Melt 2 tablespoons butter in a skillet and sauté the nettles for 5 minutes.

Put them in the blender with 5-6 mint leaves, the eggs, a generous handful each of grated parmesan cheese and breadcrumbs, salt and pepper. Blend until the mixture is nice and thick. Shape the mixture into tangerine-size balls and set them aside for 30 minutes. Now, take the little balls and roll them into sticks, cut pieces about 2-3 (1 inch) long. Sprinkle them with flour before you cook them in salted boiling water. As they float to the top remove them with a slotted spoon and put them into a bowl.

While the gnocchi cook, melt the rest of the butter in a skillet and wilt 4-5 sage leaves. Pour over the

🍴 ⏲ 20'+30' ❋ 25' 4 ★✦

600g/1.5 lb. Tender
 nettle leaves
Flour
Grated parmesan
 cheese
2 Eggs
Mint
Sage
Breadcrumbs
80g/3 oz Butter

Kcal 306 P 10 F 19

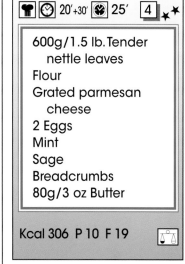

gnocchi and add two big handfuls of grated parmesan cheese.

Bread gnocchi

In a bowl, mix together the breadcrumbs, 3 tablespoons grated parmesan cheese, 2 tablespoons flour, a pinch of salt, pepper and a dash of ground nutmeg.

Blend in the eggs, the yolks and 50g/2 oz melted butter. Set the mixture aside (it should be firm because otherwise the gnocchi will dissolve as they cook) for about 1 hour. Shape nutsize balls and sprinkle with flour.

Cook in salted water and use a slotted spoon to remove them as they float to the top.

While they are still hot dress with 50g/2 oz melted butter flavored with

🍴 ⏲ 20'+1h ❋ 45' 4 ★✦

350g/13 oz
 Breadcrumbs
2 Eggs and 2 yolks
Grated parmesan
 cheese
Milk
Flour
Sage
Ground nutmeg
100 g/4 oz Butter

Kcal 629 P 41 F 46

4-5 sage leaves and grated parmesan cheese or with a tasty vegetable sauce.

Clean and chop together one carrot and one stalk celery. Clean an onion and slice it thinly. Sauté in a saucepan with 3-4 tablespoons olive oil, add the chopped carrot and celery and a pinch of coarse salt. Moisten with half a glass of broth and cook over a low flame for 10 minutes. Add 2-3 lades of tomato puré and cook very slowly, at the last minute add a sprig of parsley or basil – this is a delicious, yet light vegetable sauce.

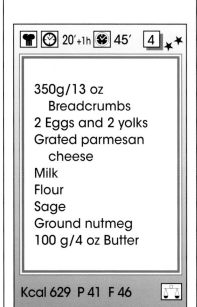

Green and white lasagne

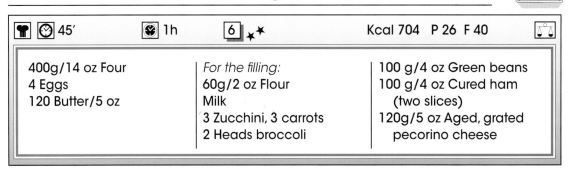

| 🍴 ⏲ 45′ | ❀ 1h | 6 ★✸ | Kcal 704 P 26 F 40 | ⚖ |

400g/14 oz Four	*For the filling:*	100 g/4 oz Green beans
4 Eggs	60g/2 oz Flour	100 g/4 oz Cured ham
120 Butter/5 oz	Milk	(two slices)
	3 Zucchini, 3 carrots	120g/5 oz Aged, grated
	2 Heads broccoli	pecorino cheese

1 Prepare the dough (see page 85) and set it aside to rest. Scald the vegetables and chop them coarsely. Melt half the butter in a saucepan, blend in 3-4 tablespoons flour and over a low flame, gradually add 2 and a half glasses milk to make the béchamel sauce. Salt to taste.

3 Roll out the dough and cut into strips 8 x 14 cm (3 x 5 inches). Cook them to the *al dente* point in salted water with a few drops of olive oil; remove with a skimmer and dry on a clean dish towel. Arrange a layer of lasagna noodles in a buttered oven dish, cover with the filling and a dusting of grated pecorino cheese.

2 Cut the ham slices into strips and brown in a skillet with 40g/1.5 oz melted butter. Add the vegetables and let them absorb the flavors. Turn off the flame and cook to lukewarm, then add 3-4 tablespoons béchamel.

4 Continue making layers until you have used up all the ingredients. Cover the top layer with the béchamel that you had set aside.
Sprinkle with grated pecorino and bake at 180°C (350°F) for barely 30 minutes.

Green lasagne

| 🍴 ⏱ 30′ | ❀ 6′+5′ | 4 ★★ | | Kcal 643 P 45 F 32 | ⚖ |

300g/12 oz Flour
3 Eggs
300g/12 oz Fresh spinach
	250g/8 oz Ricotta cheese
	Vegetable broth
	  (see page 51)
		Ground nutmeg
		Meat sauce
		  (see pages 86-87)

Prepare the green lasagna dough (see below) and set it aside to rest for a half hour. Soften the ricotta cheese in a bowl, with a fork add a pinch of salt, pepper, ground nutmeg and half a glass of broth. Roll out the dough and cut it into 10 x 20 cm (4 x 8 inches) strips. Cook them to the *al dente* point in salted water with a few drops of olive oil; remove with a skimmer and dry on a clean dish towel. As the noodles are cooked place them on a serving dish; cover with the meat sauce and spoon on the ricotta.

Whether or not to add grated parmesan cheese is up to you, either way, this is delicious.

1 Clean the spinach and scald in slightly salted water. Drain, and squeeze out the excess water.

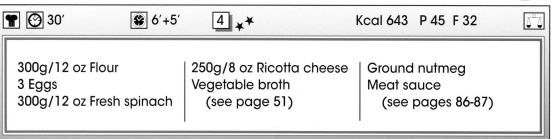

3 Put the spinach balls into the blender and chop finely at low speed.

2 Grasp a handful at a time, squeeze out the excess water and shape into balls; let the balls dry on a clean dish towel.

4 When you start making the noodles, add the spinach to the mounded flour along with the eggs and then continue following the instructions on page 85.

To make this appetizing "open" lasagna, you need good meat sauce.
Prepare it ahead of time, following the recipe on pages 86-87.

For the lasagna you will need about 3 cups – in this case *melius abundare or more is better* as the ancient Romans used to say.

Pansotti with walnuts

Make the dough by combining the flour with a glass of lukewarm water, a pinch of salt and a dash of ground nutmeg. Set it aside to rest for 30 minutes. Soak the bread in water. Scald the nuts and remove the skins. Clean the vegetables and herbs; put them into a bowl of clean water, remove drain without drying and then put them into a saucepan. Salt slightly, cover and cook over a low flame for 20 minutes. Drain, squeeze out the excess water and put into the blender with the ricotta, the whole egg and the yolk, 60g/2 oz grated parmesan cheese, another pinch of salt and 1 tablespoon olive oil. Mix at low speed. Put the mixture into a bowl and set it aside for 30 minutes. Squeeze out the bread, and put it in the blender with the nuts, 1 clove garlic and a pinch of salt, add the yogurt and mix at low speed. Put this sauce into a bowl and combine with a little less than a full glass of olive oil. Set aside. Roll out the dough, making 2 not-too-thin sheets. Distribute little heaps of the filling on one sheet, about 7-8 cm (2 1/2- 3 inches) apart; lay the other sheet of dough over it, pressing down between the filling. Use a scalloped, oblong cookie cutter (about 5 cm/ 2 inches in diameter) and make the pansotti. You can also use the pasta cutter wheel. Sprinkle with flour and cook in boiling water; use a slotted spoon to remove them as they float to the top, drain and dress with the walnut sauce and grated parmesan cheese.

🍴 🕐 1h+40′ ❀ 35′ 4 ★-★

350g/13 oz Flour
Ground nutmeg
300g/12 oz Shelled
   walnuts
1 Clove garlic
2 Slices of dry bread,
   without the crust
Grated parmesan
   cheese
3-4 Tablespoons
   yogurt
Olive oil

For the filling:
150g/6 oz Ricotta
   cheese
3-4 Bunches fresh beet
   greens
3-4 Bunches fresh
   spinach
1 Thick slice of
   cabbage
1 Bunch radicchio
Borage and
   salvastrella leaves
1 Egg and 1 yolk
Parsley

Kcal 629 P 41 F 46 ⚖

Pappardelle with mutton

Prepare the dough (see page 85) and set it aside to rest.

Clean the carrot, onion and celery, chop finely and sauté in a saucepan with 4-5 tablespoons olive oil and the bouquet. Add the meat, brown it, add half a glass of wine and let it evaporate. Salt, add the tomato purée and cook for 20 minutes, adding a little broth if it tends to dry. Clean the mushrooms with a brush, wipe them clean with a damp cloth. Cut them into chunks.

Remove the bouquet from the sauce and add the mushrooms and cook for another 10 minutes; turn off the flame.

Roll out the dough into wide strips (see page 89) and cut these into smaller strips about 3 cm (a little more than 1 inch) wide using the pasta cutter to get zigzag edges.

Cook the noodles until they are not quite *al dente*, drain and turn them into the pan with the sauce, stir and serve on plates decorated with rosemary.

Even though the word pappardelle *is in dialect, it is now commonly used even outside Tuscany for egg noodles – (home- or factory-made) that are ideal for hearty sauces, especially those made with game.*

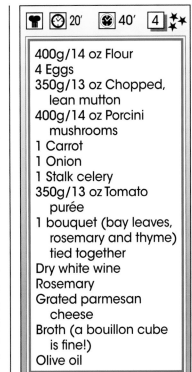

🍽 ⏱ 20′ ❄ 40′ 4 ✦✦✦

400g/14 oz Flour
4 Eggs
350g/13 oz Chopped, lean mutton
400g/14 oz Porcini mushrooms
1 Carrot
1 Onion
1 Stalk celery
350g/13 oz Tomato purée
1 bouquet (bay leaves, rosemary and thyme) tied together
Dry white wine
Rosemary
Grated parmesan cheese
Broth (a bouillon cube is fine!)
Olive oil

Kcal 674 P 38 F 34

Pappardelle with duck

Prepare the dough (see page 85) and set it aside. Dice the ham. Cut the duck into pieces.

Chop the carrot, onion and celery and sauté in a saucepan with 3-4 tablespoons olive oil, sage, rosemary and the diced ham. Add the duck and brown it, moisten with half a glass of wine and let the wine evaporate.

Salt, pour in the tomato purée, cover and cook slowly for 45 minutes, adding broth now and then if it tends to dry. Remove the duck from the pan and bone; chop the meat and put it back into the sauce and cook, uncovered for 15 minutes.

Roll out the dough and use the wheel (see page 89) to cut pappardelle.

Cook in salted water with a few drops of olive oil, drain and dress with the duck sauce. Distribute on individual plates and

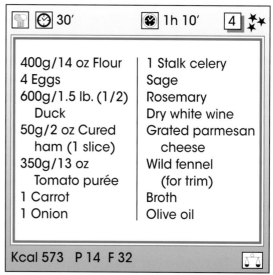

🍴 ⏱ 30′	❀ 1h 10′	4 ✦✦
400g/14 oz Flour	1 Stalk celery	
4 Eggs	Sage	
600g/1.5 lb. (1/2) Duck	Rosemary	
50g/2 oz Cured ham (1 slice)	Dry white wine	
350g/13 oz Tomato purée	Grated parmesan cheese	
1 Carrot	Wild fennel (for trim)	
1 Onion	Broth	
	Olive oil	

Kcal 573   P 14   F 32

trim with the wild fennel, but if you use grated parmesan cheese – eliminate the fennel.

Pappardelle with hare sauce

The hare must be skinned, washed, dried and cut into pieces. Place it in a bowl to marinate for 3-4 hours with the wine, vinegar, sliced carrot, onion and celery, the herbs, 3 juniper berries and black pepper corns. Prepare the dough (see page 85) and set it aside.

Scoop the vegetables out of the marinade and put them in the blender, then sauté the mixture in a saucepan with 3-4 tablespoons olive oil; add the hare and let it brown over a high flame. Pour 1/2 glass of marinade over it and let it evaporate. Salt, add the tomato purée, cover and cook over a low flame for 45 minutes, adding a little marinade now and then if it tends to dry or stick. Remove the hare from the pan and bone; chop the meat and put it back to cook uncovered for another 15 minutes. Roll out the dough and use the wheel (see page 89) to cut pappardelle. Cook in salted water with a few drops of olive oil, drain and dress with the hare sauce. Distribute on individual plates and trim with sprigs of fresh thyme.

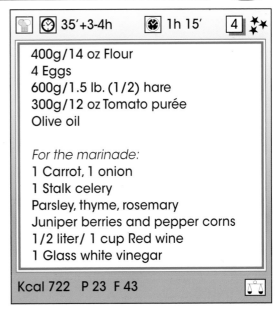

🕐 35'+3-4h	⚜ 1h 15'	4 ✦✦

400g/14 oz Flour
4 Eggs
600g/1.5 lb. (1/2) hare
300g/12 oz Tomato purée
Olive oil

For the marinade:
1 Carrot, 1 onion
1 Stalk celery
Parsley, thyme, rosemary
Juniper berries and pepper corns
1/2 liter/ 1 cup Red wine
1 Glass white vinegar

Kcal 722   P 23   F 43

Ravioli with green beans ▶

🍽 ⏰ 45' ❀ 20' 4 ⭐✦

300g/12 oz Flour
3 Eggs
350g/13 oz Green
    beans
60g/2 oz Butter

For the filling:
2 Potatoes
2 Eggs
100 g/4 oz Ricotta
Breadcrumbs
Fresh mint
Ground nutmeg
Grated parmesan
    cheese
Olive oil

Kcal 772 P 25 F 44 ⚖

Prepare the dough (see page 85) and set it aside. Boil the potatoes in the jackets, cool and peel. Put them in the blender with the ricotta, eggs, mint, a handful of breadcrumbs, salt and pepper and a dash of ground nutmeg. Mix and then set aside.

Roll out the dough into wide strips that (see page 89), use the wheel to cut 5 x 10 cm (2 x 4 inches) rectangles (see steps 3 and 4 shown on page 122). On each rectangle place two little balls of filling symmetrically, fold

then over, press the edges to seal and cut in two using the wheel.

Continue until you have used up all the ingredients. Dust the ravioli with flour.

Wash the green beans and boil them in salted water, when they are just about done, add the ravioli to the water.

As soon as the ravioli float to the top, drain and put them in a bowl, top with the drained beans and garnish with butter and mint leaves. Serve with a sprinkling of grated parmesan cheese.

Two-flavor ravioli

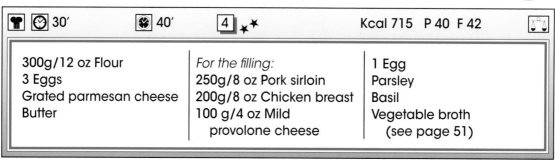

🍽 ⏰ 30' ❀ 40' 4 ⭐✦ Kcal 715 P 40 F 42 ⚖

300g/12 oz Flour	*For the filling:*	1 Egg
3 Eggs	250g/8 oz Pork sirloin	Parsley
Grated parmesan cheese	200g/8 oz Chicken breast	Basil
Butter	100 g/4 oz Mild	Vegetable broth
	provolone cheese	(see page 51)

Prepare the dough (see page 85) and set it aside.

Put the meat into a saucepan, cover it with the broth, add a pinch of salt and cook for 30 minutes.

Turn off the flame, remove the meat and cut it into small chunks.

Put the provolone into the still hot broth, and then put it into the blender with the meat, egg, parsley, basil, salt and pepper. Blend, then set aside. Roll out the dough into wide strips that (see page 89), use

the wheel to cut 5 x 10 cm (2 x 4 inch) rectangles (see steps 3 and 4 shown on page 122). On each rectangle place two little balls of filling symmetrically, fold them over, press the edges to seal and cut in two using the wheel.

Continue until you have used up all the ingredients.

Dust the ravioli with flour and cook in salted boiling water.

Drain and dress with 50g/2 oz butter and lots of grated parmesan cheese.

An alternative to ravioli? How about crespelle (or filled crêpes). Beat 2 eggs in a bowl, add 200g/8 oz flour and a glass of milk. Stir with a whisk gradually adding 3 more glasses of milk, a little melted butter and a pinch of salt. Set aside for 1 hour. Melt a pat of butter in a pan, and pour on some of the batter. When the batter is set, flip it over.

Fill the crêpes with your favorite filling (such as ricotta and spinach) and bake for 10 minutes.

Green ravioli

Prepare the green dough using 300g/12 oz flour according to the instructions on page 102 and set it aside for a half hour. Melt 30g/1 oz butter in a saucepan and gradually blend in the rest of the flour.

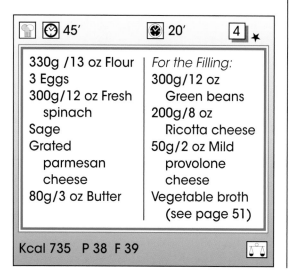

	⏱ 45'	✦ 20'	4 ★

330g /13 oz Flour	*For the Filling:*
3 Eggs	300g/12 oz
300g/12 oz Fresh	Green beans
spinach	200g/8 oz
Sage	Ricotta cheese
Grated	50g/2 oz Mild
parmesan	provolone
cheese	cheese
80g/3 oz Butter	Vegetable broth
	(see page 51)

Kcal 735   P 38   F 39

Slowly add the vegetable broth, stirring all the while to make a thick white or (*velouté*) sauce. Clean the green beans and cook them *al dente* in boiling salted water. Put them into the blender with the ricotta, grated provolone cheese and a dash of salt. Blend, add the white sauce and set aside.

Roll out the dough into wide strips that (see page 89), use the when to cut 5 x 10 cm (2 x 4 inches) rectangles (see steps 3 and 4 shown on page 122).

On each rectangle place two little balls of filling symmetrically, fold then over, press the edges to seal and cut in two using the wheel. Continue until you have used up all the ingredients. Dust the ravioli with flour and cook in salted boiling water. Drain and dress with 50g/2 oz butter and lots of grated parmesan cheese.

Ravioli in ginger sauce

Mound the flour on the work table, break the yolks into it, and combine with the baking powder, and a dash of salt; knead gradually adding a glass of lukewarm water. Cover the dough with a cloth and set it aside for 1 hour.

Clean the cabbage, separate the leaves and scald it. Put it in the blender with all the other filling ingredients and blend until the mixture is smooth and malleable. Put it into a bowl and blend in 1 tablespoon cold water.

Roll out the dough thinly and cut 12 cm (5 inches) disks, use up all the scraps of dough too. Put some of filling into the middle of each disk shape into little bundles, pressing the edges to seal.

Steam cook in the special basket (you may have to cook 2 batches) for 20 minutes. Combine 4 slices of ginger with a

small bowl of vinegar and mix until it becomes an homogeneous sauce; pour the sauce over the hot ravioli.

⏱ 40'+1h	✦ 20'	4 ★★

250g/8 oz Flour	250g/8 oz
Baking powder	Chinese or
2 Egg yolks	plain cabbage
Fresh ginger	Soy sauce
Red vinegar	Sugar
	Corn starch
For the filling:	Black pepper
1 Shallot	
1 Clove garlic	

Kcal 488   P 10   F 25

The traditional filling for ravioli is made with ricotta cheese and spinach. It seems that originally the recipe called for turnip tops, and that the word "ravioli" comes from "rabiola" the Medieval diminutive of the Italian word for turnip top, that is rapa. There are variations in making the dough, rather than changing the filling. Boil 200g/8 oz of beets and 1 carrot; combine in the blender and make a paste and add it to the flour as you prepare the dough. The ravioli will, obviously, be pink and you can fill them with meat combined with savoy cabbage, lettuce, endive and herbs – amazing!

Ravioli southern style

Prepare the dough using 300g/12 oz flour (see page 85) and set it aside. Melt 30g/1 oz butter in a saucepan and slowly add the rest of the flour. Gradually add 1 glass of vegetable broth, stirring all the while to make a thick, white sauce. Combine with the meat sauce.

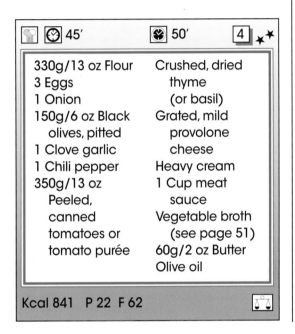

🕐 45′	✿ 50′	4 ★✶
330g/13 oz Flour	Crushed, dried	
3 Eggs	thyme	
1 Onion	(or basil)	
150g/6 oz Black	Grated, mild	
olives, pitted	provolone	
1 Clove garlic	cheese	
1 Chili pepper	Heavy cream	
350g/13 oz	1 Cup meat	
Peeled,	sauce	
canned	Vegetable broth	
tomatoes or	(see page 51)	
tomato purée	60g/2 oz Butter	
	Olive oil	

Kcal 841   P 22   F 62

Chop the onion and garlic together and sauté in a saucepan with 4-5 tablespoons olive oil and the crushed chili pepper. Add the tomatoes, salt and pepper and a dash of thyme (or if you prefer, 4-5 chopped basil leaves). Cook over a medium flame for about 20 minutes, then put it through the food mill (small holes). Put the sauce back into the pan, add the olives and simmer for about 5 minutes. Roll out the dough into wide strips that (see page 89), use the wheel to cut 5 x 10 cm (2 x 4 inches) rectangles (see steps 3 and 4 shown on page 122). On each rectangle place two little balls of filling symmetrically, fold then over, press the edges to seal and cut in two using the wheel. Continue until you have used up all the ingredients. Dust the ravioli with flour and cook in salted boiling water. Drain and put the ravioli into a buttered oven dish. Dress with the sauce and cream; bake at 180°-220°C (350°-430°F) for just 10 minutes. Sprinkle generously with grated mild provolone cheese and serve hot.

Striscioni with thyme

Prepare the dough (see page 85) and set it aside. Wash the thyme leaves, dry them well and put them in the blender with a handful of grated parmesan cheese and a pinch of salt and pepper. Set the mixture aside. Roll out the dough and cut uneven strips (see page 89) ranging from 2 to 4 cm (1 to 2 inches) wide. Cook the noodles in boiling salted water with a few drops of olive oil. In the meantime, melt the butter in a skillet along with barely a ladle of hot vegetable broth. Drain the noodles and turn them into the pan, turn off the flame and add the thyme mixture. Mix well and serve with a generous amount of grated parmesan cheese.

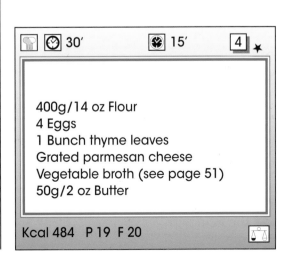

🕐 30′	✿ 15′	4 ★
400g/14 oz Flour		
4 Eggs		
1 Bunch thyme leaves		
Grated parmesan cheese		
Vegetable broth (see page 51)		
50g/2 oz Butter		

Kcal 484   P 19   F 20

Springtime noodle loaf

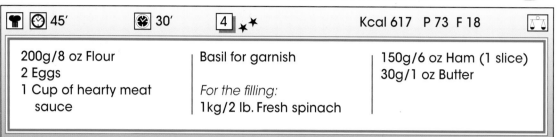

🍳 ⏰ 45′	❄ 30′	4 ★⋆★		Kcal 617 P 73 F 18	⚖

200g/8 oz Flour 2 Eggs 1 Cup of hearty meat sauce	Basil for garnish *For the filling:* 1kg/2 lb. Fresh spinach	150g/6 oz Ham (1 slice) 30g/1 oz Butter

To make the meat sauce, follow the instructions on pages 86-87, but make sure to add a chopped shallot, a few sage leaves and a sprig of rosemary to the basic vegetables and herbs.

3 Roll out the dough in a single sheet, about 18 x 35 cm (7 x 14 inches) that should not be too thin. Place the filling in the middle and roll it into a loaf.

1 Prepare the dough (see page 85) and set it aside. Clean the spinach and scald it in a little salted water, drain and squeeze out the water. Dice the ham and brown it in a skillet with the melted butter.

2 Finely chop the spinach and add it to the ham with a dash of salt. Cook for 4-5 minutes.

4 Roll the loaf in a clean dish cloth and tie with string. Place it in an appropriately shaped pot and cook for 20 minutes in salted water. Remove it from the pot, take off the string and cloth and put the loaf on a serving dish. Slice, dress with the meat sauce and garnish with sprigs of basil. Grated parmesan cheese is optional.

The egg-flour ratio for making tagliatelle, fettuccine, etc, is usually 1 egg for every 100 g/4 oz flour and is based on the culinary dictates of the Emilia-Romagna region where egg pasta is king – this does not mean to detract from other parts of Italy, but... These are hearty proportions if you consider that you can even use 1 egg for every 200g/8 oz flour, this yields a lighter dough that is suitable for diets.

Tagliatelle with ham

Prepare the dough (see page 85) and set it aside. Clean and slice the carrot and onion and sauté in a saucepan with 3 tablespoons olive oil. Cut the ham into strips and brown it in the vegetables, add the tomatoes, salt (just a little because the ham is quite salty) and cook over a medium flame for 15 minutes.

Roll out the dough and cut the tagliatelle 1 cm (1/2) wide. Cook the noodles in salted water, with a few drops of olive oil until they are *al dente*, drain and dress with the ham sauce and lots of grated parmesan cheese.

🍴 ⏱ 35' ⏲ 30' 4 ✶✶

400g/14 oz Flour
4 Eggs
Grated parmesan
cheese

For the sauce:
150g/6 oz Cured ham
350g/13 oz Canned,
peeled tomatoes
1 Onion
1 Carrot
Rosemary
Olive oil

Kcal 683 P 21 F 41

Strascinati with lamb sauce

Strascinati *come from the Puglia and Basilicata regions. The dough is quite literally dragged along a rough wooden board so that the surface becomes uneven. Strascinati should be made a day ahead of time, but you can find them quite easily – ready-made and packaged. The traditional recipe calls for a sauce made with mutton, but we have opted for lamb which is milder.*

Blend the flour with the 20g/1 oz of lard and a pinch salt, gradually adding lukewarm water. Set aside for a little while, then roll out the dough in wide strips, cut lozenges about 4-5 cm (2-2 1/2 inches on a side). Press them onto a fine sieve or the back of a fine grater. Cover with two clean cloths set them aside to dry thoroughly. Chop together the onion and garlic, sauté in a saucepan with 3-4 tablespoons olive oil and the diced bacon. Cut the meat into little chunks and brown it in the onion and garlic; moisten with half a glass of wine and let the wine evaporate. Add the tomato purée, a pinch of salt and of ground chili pepper. Cover and cook over a very low flame for 45 minutes; add a couple of ladles of vegetable broth as needed. Uncover and cook for another 15 minutes. Cook the pasta in lots of salted water, drain and dress with the sauce. Top with chopped parsley and grated parmesan cheese and serve hot.

🍴 ⏱ 35' ⏲ 1h 15' 4 ✶✶✶

400g/14 oz Flour
20g/1 oz Lard
Parsley
Aged, grated pecorino
cheese

For the sauce:
300g/12 oz Lean lamb
1/2 Onion, 1 clove garlic
Ground chili pepper
350g/13 oz Tomato purée
50g/2 oz Bacon or
fatback
Red wine, olive oil
Vegetable broth
(see page 51)

Kcal 857 P 20 F 60

Tagliolini timbale ▶

🍴 ⏱ 25′	✿ 35′	4 ★		Kcal 666 P 29 F 43	⚖
350g/13 oz Flour 5 Eggs		100 g/4 oz Butter 2 Glasses milk		200g/8 oz Ham Grated parmesan chees	

If you want to a very special touch fill the center of the timbale with mushrooms sautéd in butter and parsley.

1 Prepare the dough using 300g/12 oz flour and 3 eggs (see page 85) and set it aside. Dice the big piece of ham. Beat the remaining eggs in a bowl and mix in the diced ham, a handful of grated parmesan cheese, salt and pepper.

2 Roll out the dough and cut tagliolini (see page 89). Cook the noodles *al dente* in salted water with a few drops of olive oil, drain and turn into the bowl with the ham, egg and cheese mixture.

3 Melt 40g/1.5 oz butter in a saucepan, over a very low flame blend in the rest of the flour – stirring in the same direction all the while – and a pinch of salt, then add the milk, a little at a time. Combine the béchamel sauce with the noodles.

4 Butter a tube pan and arrange the noodle mixture, sprinkle with breadcrumbs and a little melted butter. Press down and bake at 180°C (350°F) for 20 minutes. Turn the timbale onto a serving platter, garnish with 3 slices of ham and slice into wedges.

Vincisgrassi

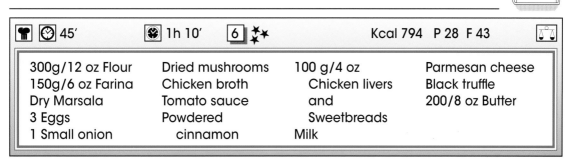

| 🍴 ⏱ 45′ | ⚙ 1h 10′ | 6 ✦★ | Kcal 794 P 28 F 43 | ⚖ |

300g/12 oz Flour	Dried mushrooms	100 g/4 oz	Parmesan cheese
150g/6 oz Farina	Chicken broth	Chicken livers	Black truffle
Dry Marsala	Tomato sauce	and	200/8 oz Butter
3 Eggs	Powdered	Sweetbreads	
1 Small onion	cinnamon	Milk	

Soak the mushrooms in lukewarm water; clean the sweetbreads and chicken livers. Prepare the dough using 250g/8 oz flour and the eggs (see page 85), blend in the farina, a dab of butter and about 2 tablespoons Marsala and set it aside for 30 minutes. Drain the mushrooms, squeeze out the excess water and chop. Clean and slice the onion, sauté in a saucepan with 30g/1 oz butter. Add a ladle of broth; add the mushrooms and after a few minutes, the tomatoes, salt and pepper, a dash of cinnamon and cook over a low flame for 10 minutes more.

See the instructions on the opposite page for béchamel sauce, but use 30g/1 oz butter, 4 tablespoons flour, a pinch of salt, and a not quite full glass of milk (this sauce will be thicker). Pour the béchamel into the tomato and mushroom mixture along with another ladle of broth, cook for 2-3 minutes. Melt 30g/1 oz butter in a skillet and brown the chopped up sweetbreads and chicken livers. Roll out the dough and cut it into 10 x 25 cm (4 x 9 inches) strips. Cook the noodles *al dente* (about 6 minutes) in salted water with a few drops of olive oil. Remove them with a slotted spoon and lay them on a cloth to dry. Butter an oven dish and make a layer of noodles, cover with the tomato sauce, lots of grated parmesan cheese, part of the sweetbread and chicken liver mixture, a few slices of truffle and dot with butter; continue making layers until you have used up all the ingredients and then top with the béchamel sauce. Bake at 180°C (350°F) for 30 minutes.

Gourmet's timbale

This is another dish that requires a good meat sauce; follow the recipe on pages 86/87.

	⏲ 40'	❀ 25'	4	★★

340g/13 oz Flour
3 Eggs
300g/12 oz Fresh spinach

For the filling:
1 Cup meat sauce
40g/1.5 oz Butter
Vegetable broth
70g/2 oz Emmenthal cheese
Black truffle

Kcal 692 P 38 F 37

Prepare the green dough (see page 102) using 300g/12 oz flour and set it aside for 30 minutes. Grate the Emmenthal cheese.

Melt 40g/1.5 oz butter in a saucepan, blend in the rest of the flour, stirring in the same direction all the while, add a pinch of salt and gradually add the broth. Cook over a low flame until the sauce thickens and blend in the cheese. Roll out the dough and then cut 8 x 14 cm (3 x 5 inches) strips.

Cook the noodles *al dente* in salted water with a few drops of olive oil; remove with a slotted spoon and place on a dry cloth. Butter an oven dish, place a layer of noodles on the bottom, cover with sauce, then with the white sauce and truffle slices. Keep on making layers like this until you have used up all the ingredients, ending with a top layer of white sauce. Bake at 200°C (400°F) for 10 minutes.

Tortelli with squash filling

Prepare the dough (see page 85) and set it aside. Boil the potato in the jacket, cool and peel. Peel the squash, remove the seeds and cut it into chunks. Melt 40g/1.5 oz butter in a skillet and sauté the squash.

Then, put the squash into the blender along with the potato, grated parmesan cheese, the biscuits, the egg and the yolk, a dash of ground nutmeg and a pinch of salt.

Roll out the dough into wide strips that are not too thin, use the wheel to cut 5 x 10 cm (2 x 4 inches) rectangles (see steps 3 and 4 shown on page 122).

On each rectangle place two little balls of filling symmetrically, fold then over, press the edges to seal and cut in two using the wheel. Continue until you have used up all the ingredients. Dust the tortelli with flour. Cook in salted water, drain and dress with butter and lots of grated parmesan cheese.

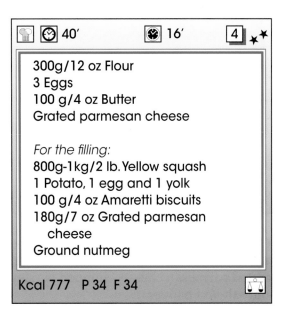

🍳 ⏱ 40′	✳ 16′	4 ★★

300g/12 oz Flour
3 Eggs
100 g/4 oz Butter
Grated parmesan cheese

For the filling:
800g-1kg/2 lb. Yellow squash
1 Potato, 1 egg and 1 yolk
100 g/4 oz Amaretti biscuits
180g/7 oz Grated parmesan cheese
Ground nutmeg

Kcal 777   P 34   F 34

Tortelli with potato filling

🍴 ⏱ 40′   ❀ 16′   4 ★★

300g/12 oz Flour
4 Eggs and 1 yolk
500g/1 lb. Potatoes
80g/3 oz Grated parmesan cheese
Parsley
Meat sauce (see pages 86-87)

Kcal 660   P 27   F 34

3 Use the wheel to cut 5 x 10 cm (2 x 4 inches) rectangles. On each rectangle place two little balls of filling symmetrically, fold then over, and cut in two using the wheel. Continue until you have used up all the ingredients.

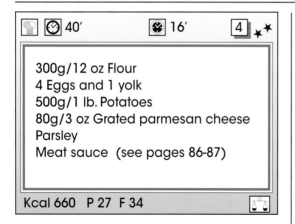

1 Prepare the dough using 3 eggs (see page 85) and set it aside for 30 minutes. Roll out the dough, making wide strips and put them on a cloth. Boil the potatoes in the jackets, cool and peel. Put them through the ricer.

4 Press the edges firmly to seal. Dust the tortelli with flour. Cook in salted water, drain and dress with meat sauce (see pages 86-87) and lots of grated parmesan cheese.

2 Put the potatoes into a bowl and use a wooden spoon to blend in the egg, grated parmesan cheese, chopped parsley and salt and pepper.

The procedure for making tortelli, *as shown in steps 3 and 4 on this page is applicable to every other similarly shaped pasta including* agnolotti, raviolini, ravioli, vincisgrassi *and so forth, as you can see in the individual recipes.*

Tortelli in broth

You make the broth, for these tortelli *by boiling half a capon for 90 minutes with carrot, onion, celery, one tomato and a pinch of salt. Or you can make a combination broth, start with beef, the same vegetables and then, after about 45 minutes, add half a pullet.*

Prepare the dough (see page 85) and set it aside. Clean the beet greens, boil them, drain and squeeze out the excess water. Rinse the calf's brain under water, remove the outer skin and scald. Melt 30g/1 oz butter in a saucepan and brown the chopped meat. Put the meat into the blender with the calf's brain, beet greens, egg, grated parmesan cheese, a dash of nutmeg, salt and pepper. Roll out the dough use the wheel to cut 5 x 10 cm (2 x 4 inches) rectangles (see steps 3 and 4 shown on page 122). On each rectangle place two little balls of filling symmetrically, fold then over, press the edges to seal and cut in two using the wheel. Continue until you have used up all the ingredients. Dust the tortelli with flour and cook them in the broth. Serve with a sprinkling of grated parmesan cheese.

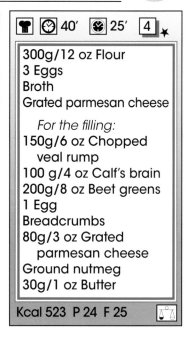

| 🍽 | ⏲ 40′ | ✸ 25′ | 4 | ★ |

300g/12 oz Flour
3 Eggs
Broth
Grated parmesan cheese

For the filling:
150g/6 oz Chopped veal rump
100 g/4 oz Calf's brain
200g/8 oz Beet greens
1 Egg
Breadcrumbs
80g/3 oz Grated parmesan cheese
Ground nutmeg
30g/1 oz Butter

Kcal 523   P 24   F 25

Rich tortellini

Prepare the dough (see page 85) and set it aside. Clean the vegetables and put them in a saucepan filled with salted water. When the water boils put in the pigeon and turkey breast.

Cook for about 20 minutes, turn off the flame and let it cool to lukewarm. Put the meats into the blender with the ham, egg yolk 4-5 tablespoons grated parmesan cheese, the stracchino, and salt and pepper. Blend, then set the mixture aside to rest. Roll out the dough, use the wheel to cut 3 x 5 cm (1 1/2 x 2 inches) rectangles (see page 126).

Place a little ball of filling in the middle of each, fold over and press the edges with your fingers to seal. Then shape the tortellini by folding them around your index finger (or pinky).

Cook for about 10 minutes in salted water, drain and dress with butter and grated parmesan cheese if you like.

🍴 ⏱ 40' ❀ 40' 4 ★★

300g/12 oz Flour
3 Eggs

For the filling:
1/2 Pigeon, boned
100 g/4 oz Turkey
    breast
100 g/4 oz Cured ham
1 Egg yolk
80g/3 oz Stracchino
    cheese
Grated parmesan
    cheese
1/2 Carrot
1/2 Onion
1/2 Stalk celery

Kcal 596 P 38 F 30 ⚖

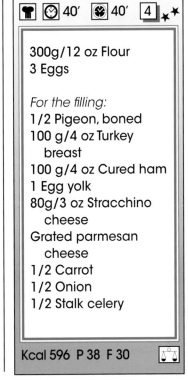

Classic tortellini

🍳 ⏱ 40′	❀ 40′	6 ★✦	Kcal 675 P 40 F 31	⚖

400g/14 oz Flour 4 Eggs *For the filling:* 150g/6 oz Veal rump	150g/6 oz Pork sirloin 50g/2 oz Mortadella 2 Slices cured ham 50g/2 oz Turkey breast 200g/8 oz Calf's liver	Grated parmesan cheese 2 Egg yolks Ground nutmeg 30g/1 oz Butter

1 Prepare the dough (see page 85) and set it aside. Rinse the calf's brain under running water and remove the skin. Melt the butter in a saucepan and brown the meats, cold cuts and brain for about 6-7 minutes. Put the contents of the pan into the blender along with the egg yolks, 100 g/4 oz grated parmesan cheese, salt and pepper and a dash of ground nutmeg. Roll out wide strips of dough and then use the wheel to cut 3 x 5 cm (1 1/2 x 2 inch) rectangles.

3 Fold over and press the edges with your fingers to seal and place on a dry dish towel.

4 Shape the tortellini by folding them around your index finger (or pinky). Cook for about 10 minutes in salted water, drain and dress with tasty meat sauce.

2 Place a little ball of filling, about the size of a hazelnut in the middle of each.

You can store tortellini *for a week or more, by keeping them in a dry place, between two dish clothes, making sure that they do not touch* each other. *In fact* tortellini *are generally prepared at least one day before they are used. If you want to cook and serve them in broth* (which must absolutely be capon broth), they should be quite a bit smaller than the ones for eating with meat or butter toppings.